LIFE

In The Key of

A-FLAT

Written By

Michael Portley, Jr.

ISBN 979-8-88862-184-4

PREFACE AND ACKNOWLEDGEMENT

What inspired me to write this book was that as I get older the elements of life experiences in detail seem to drift and are merely left to memory which becomes vague over time. Another reason was that my two favorite prophets Elijah and Elisha had no literature. They were oral prophets, not literary prophets. This simply means that they provided direction spiritually but without the tutelage of documentation scholastically.

Also St. John the beloved Apostle defended himself with ease and sophistication through his writing documents. In John 21:21 as St. Peter interrogated Jesus about John's mission asking him "what shall this man do". John was writing which gave him authoritative control of the narrative. I always wondered what Peter would have said had he had the microphone which on that day was the pen. I never thought John misrepresented the truth, but perhaps Peter could've told his side in fuller account had he written more.

I dedicate this work to the life of my father and mother, Michael W. and Lauretta G. Portley. They are no longer with us on the earth; however, they live on through me as they instilled in me the importance of the Word of God as well as making an impact in the world as unto the glory of God. They also encouraged me musically. Though this book is not based on music it was encouraged by it. My first glance at music was my mother as she showed me my first set of chords. As a young musician when I got stuck on a song, she would often say to me "chord your way through it". I never forgot that phrase and even after her departure I'd learn to repurpose that phrase. When life got tough then I would " Pray my way through it" ``Push my way through it ```'Grind my way through it" and so on. My parents also were a motivation for me to write this book as I noticed how that beyond pictures much of their life was left undocumented. Their earthly experience though brief was much more than what the world would've assumed and even more appetizing than what pictures alone could capture, and stories could explain.

Nostalgically, there's no video tape, DVD, cassette tape, link or social media footage that enables loved ones to replay either of their final services. It's really no one's fault as me and my other siblings were all young in addition to technology not being around in mass form at the time of their passing. Moving forward this reality has always cautioned me to document meaningful moments as well as to mentally notate seasons and sessions of milestones and even hardship as they too are often ingredients that God uses to birth purpose.

A few others that I'd like to mention briefly as cornerstones of investments:

- My Spiritual Father Supt Elvin Rhone Jr of the Power Realm Ministries, love you dad, I will always honor you and Mother Betty Rhone. Also, to my former pastor, the late Elder R. Michael Copeland of New Harvest Cogic who also poured into me abundantly. Blessings to him and Lady Deborah Copeland for labor of love. Finally, I want to recognize the late Rev. Brandon McCray, my dear cousin and world-renowned saxophonist who was always a voice inspiration. I want to also recognize the leadership of Bishop Keith and Pastor Latoya Tribitt as we shared notable veins in ministry during my season with the Mica Family. I'd like to also recognize Pastor Charles and Carolyn Cofield as they fathered and mothered me a full calendar year when I organized my first pastoral work. I will always cherish and remember the sacrifice of love shown. Then there's only one Linda Cofield. I crown her as the music mentor responsible for dressing me for the ministry side of music which I am forever grateful for.

- The Transformation Family Life Center affectionately known as TFLC. This was a ministry that I was blessed to have organized some time ago. From its inception to its conclusion, it was an honor to lead, feed, intercede for and serve this parish. For 15 years prior to a change in commission for me I created many relationships that Left a long-lasting imprint upon my life. This chapter in my life was very important as it assisted in the birthing of the book as it taught me stability. I'm forever grateful and thankful to have been able to serve such good people for the time God allowed.

- To my mother-in-love, Mother Pamela Brown, who has always been a constant support of me and my family as well as the entire Brown family, I thank you all for your continued years of support. I'd also like to recognize my spiritual mother and media mentor Apostle Dr. Marilyn Todman. I thank you and Bishop Todman for being who God called you to be and the global impact being made at PTWWN (Preach the Word WorldWide Network).

- I also want to acknowledge my siblings. I'm very delighted that all 6 of them are alive and well. We've seen tough days and have cried together, sang together, and pressed through the walls of impossibility. I honor them all. Carlton, Tifani, Preston (Erica), Monica, Kristi (Tyrone), and Ramon. I thank you all for being strong, courageous and purpose driven. I also want to mention my late godmother Missionary Elzada Mack and God-sister Rashonda for their years of support to me. Also, to my SeaCo family for years of support.

- Last but not least I want to give honor to the journal of my heart and the flagship of my inspiration, the love of my life, my wife Lady RaQeisha Portley and my son Michael W. Portley lll, aka Tre. It all starts at home. It's been an awesome privilege the last nearly 23 years to do life with you. RaQeisha Portley, you've evolved as a person, and you've allowed me to do so as well. Your support for me and our son has been amazing, as well as your grace, your goodness, and your glow! RaQeisha I love you dearly. Thank You for your willingness to understand my call and all that comes with it. You've made me a better man. Consistent you are and faithful you've been. To my son and only child Tre. Son, dad loves you unconditionally. I'm proud of who you are and how you've allowed God to be seen in and through you. Dad loves you. May I also thank my publishers Lead Press Corporations for their trust in me and making the process enjoyable. You all are the real deal as you've allowed me to unlock the hidden treasures of book writing. May God continue to bless you all.

FOREWORD

"Life In the Key Of A-Flat" is an amazing book to aide anyone who is seeking direction in their journey of life. Life as we know can get discouraging and complicated, but there is hope for those who read this book.

Pastor Michael Portley reinforces the necessity of Faith, Fortitude and Freedom and ignites the reader to a place of restoration and empowerment.

This work comes from the heart of God and through the man of God for the people of God.

This book is a must read for anyone who desires to advance in spiritual truths and revelation knowledge.

You are in for a treat as I know you will be blessed.

Dr. Marilyn Todman

CEO of PTWWN Broadcasting Inc.

CHAPTER 1

Using the Faith in A-Flat to overcome the Fears of A-natural

I will start this book the way we started out what was called "testimony service" in the Holiness church. It went like this… *"First giving honor to God who is the head of my life, and to the pastor, members' friends, Saints and aint's, God loves you."* Then we would transition it like this…. *"I'm so glad to be in the number, one more time; He didn't have to let me live because millions didn't make it, but I was one of the ones who did."*

Well, I'm having a testimonial moment as God has allowed me to write this book as a tool of encouragement and a tablet of inspiration for Enlightenment, Enrichment and Empowerment. We live in "A" day that's very chaotic and extremely tentative. It seems like we're seeing the worst of times with a tentative promise that it will only get worse. With this in mind, I've decided to chronicle my life sharing notes, nuggets and knowledge that otherwise risk going uncaptured, tucked away and perhaps never spoken about again. My life isn't celebrated for what I have but rather what I've survived to tell. For many of you reading, you're like me. it's not so much what you've accomplished but how far you've gone with so little. It is in these times that we have to 'Wait' on the Lord. And what I mean by 'wait' is described by way of an acronym:

W.A.I.T.

W - Weather the storm

A - Apply what survival techniques acquired while in the storm.

I - Inspiration is key. Find sources that inspire you. Walk, run, sing, sabbath, write, laugh, love, commit, conclude, initiate and so on.

T - Time is what you need as well as what you owe God to work things out in your best interest.

A 2-year pandemic has been something we've never seen before and can also be damaging to one's hope. Especially when we look at our world consider the increasing turmoil of:

***We see the forest fires California

***Afghanistan terrorism and famine

***the 2-year sequel Covid-19 virus variants,

*** The unscheduled hurricanes in Wichita Kansas

***The Earthquakes in Haiti killing thousands,

***The deceased birds falling from the sky in New Mexico (the unclean air).

***The contaminated water in Texas

**** The nationwide shortage of baby milk formula

***The school shootings that left innocent casualties to be mourned by their loved ones.

***The augmented uptick in the food cost due to the shortages of supply.

***The ravishing inflation of gas prices and fueled by the oil shortages.

With all this unraveling right before our eyes it needs to be reinforced that our good still outweighs our bad. We must renew our hope in God and reclaim our joy. Many things have challenged my joy in this season, but it was good for me because it allowed me to distinguish the difference between happiness and joy. Happiness was based on what happened, so it's compared to a thermometer. While joy is never predicated on what happened but rather is unmoved because it is more of a thermostat.

The joy that I feel is the same joy that I'm hopeful to ignite to all those I'm assigned to touch through this work. I frequently felt joy before I was able to understand it and or described it.

In simple terms to me it is the Juice of Life, & The Center of Paradise! Its High-Octane Energy sponsored by the souls expression! Joy also is the spontaneous rush of spiritual vibration manifested through the senses! One of the joys of being Levitical Priest is the view of life vertically (in touch with Jehovah) as well as horizontally, in the earth. My prayer is this, "May the Joy of Lord be Your Strength" as you turn the pages of this book seeking to capture relevance and insight serving as beacon of light as spiritual truths through the lens of my story are shared.

While this book is not meant to be a musical rendition of theory or fundamentals. I must admit that music is a flagship of my life that has sponsored many other opportunities catapulting me into many open doors and allowing my uniqueness to be magnetic. Music for me was my birthing canal that God used for other qualities and callings to be born. It awakened me to further my purpose in this brief span called Life. We, as the human family are often in search of two things:

Day Work: How we support ourselves in relation to necessity and beyond.

Life Task: What I'm called to do, and to whom I'm called to serve.

Wisdom overtime allows the two to merge as one, allowing the savings of time as well as physical preservation on that path is discovered. For me, music was what secured my identity and because of the notice gained publicly I've grown to learn whatever else I'd set out to accomplish was mine to lose as the influence was a given. Before we explore other sectors of what my *Life in A-flat* is, let's talk A-flat!

As a seasoned music professional, I learned many years ago to play in all 12 of the keys. However, this did not come without challenges. So, A-Flat is my favorite key not because it was my only performance key but because it was a representation of my **FIRST**. Let's look at my F.I.R.S.T as an acronym.

My **FIRST, INITIAL, RESPONSE,** that **SET** the **TONE.**
Here goes the laundry list:

- The first song I wrote was for my high school graduation back in 1998. I was able to provide a new arrangement of the school song called WYANDOTTE FOREVER, named after the school "Wyandotte High School". I was able to rearrange it as the music teacher and administration approved and allowed it to be sung at the commencement celebration my

- The first series of hymns that I learned how to play were surrounded around the theme of The Blood sang on first Sundays during communion. They were all sung in the key of A-Flat.

- After a 2-week ministry sabbatical after my mom's death, I returned back to my post at my local church on a Tuesday morning preparing for rehearsal. Out of the atmosphere of the anointing I wrote my first original hymn entitled "Morning By Morning". Guess what key it was in? Yes, A-Flat!!

- Walking into my mother's homegoing celebration in 2000, the hired musician plays the procession song as we walk in "EVERYTHING WILL BE ALRIGHT " In the key of A-Flat.

- A-Flat was my mother's favorite key to sing and to play in as well. Therefore, she showed my first set of chords from the A Flat perspective.

A Flat is the average preacher's key when they close their sermon in a musical sound. It was also the key that they often go to for sound in a church scene of a movie.

An A-flat by the assumption of default is a major key with a major sound. Also like any other key, major chords are juxtaposed with minor chords. Minor chord progression does release a sound of mystery, ominous and warfare that seems to signify some sense of tension, suspense, or unsettling. Yet to be able to play in minor progression in the Pentecostal Church was seen as virtuosic and, in some ways, enigmatic. Though A Flat has a minor, theoretically A Flat minor was the same major progressions to the key of B major. It was all about placement and perspective, as is life. So even when in situations that have minor undertones of brokenness and hard trial connected to them, be encouraged that there's still a major somewhere waiting to be identified. All opposition comes packaged with an opportunity.

This reality was reinforced to me some years back when my sisters went to China with a group of music professionals. We would talk at odd hours of the day as China has a 12-hour time difference from the United States. So, when it was bedtime in the States it was daytime in China. Further studies proved that the earth was never void of light. Though dark in one geographical sphere it was light somewhere else and vice versa. Jesus really is unquestionably, the unchanging and unquenchable Light of the world; even in seemingly darkness, He still shines.

Whatever key life finds you in, whether sour or sweet, take the lemons and make lemonade. Take the aged bananas that were once yellow but now brown and make banana bread. Majors and Minors are linked to life in a variety of ways. We hate mud and despise manure. Yet there are minerals in both the mud an and manure that grows potatoes and also fortifies strength in us to endure what life throws at us. This includes the majors in sound, the majors in opportunities and platform, but also the unpreferred minors that are engulfed with.

I often observed how that in many other faith circles as well as it was with classically trained musicians, how they learned first to perfect the white keys, or what is universally recognized as the *IVORY. As one with a Pentecostal background, such as myself, the emphasis was to learn the black keys or what is universally recognized as the *EBONY. This was suggested based on the keys that the radio gospel hits were written in. The church often patterned the song selections fostering that blueprint.

While I appreciate all 12 of these keys known to music, A-natural was my least favorite key and last of the 12 that I learned. From my perspective, everyone has an A-natural possibility. Meaning that we are often one-half step away from trial even while in Triumph.

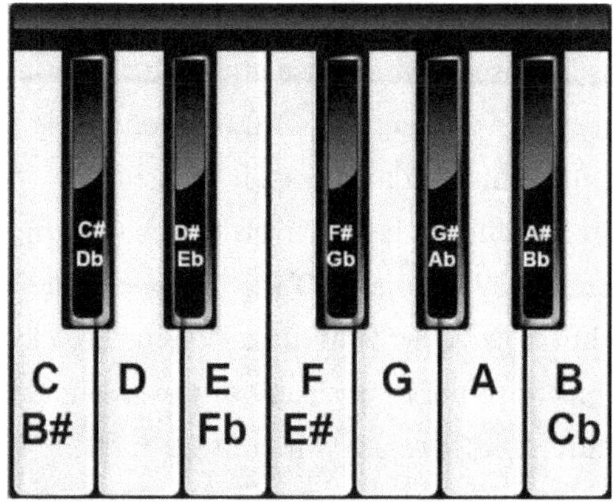

So, we must handle people with the same care and respect who are in their trial of A-natural remembering that we are just a half step away from being the one who can help apart from the one that needs the help. On the contrary, If and when life finds us enamored in natural situations of opposition, we must know that they are so close, as in one half step away from recovery, deliverance and or restoration needed.

A- Flat was also a travel agent for me. Just as the airplane expedites travel time, so did A-flat for me. It was almost like Exodus 4:19 NIV when Moses writes: *"You yourselves have seen what I did to Egypt, and how I carried you on eagles' wings and brought you to myself"*

The Eagle was likened to the airplane which was likened to A-Flat. It carried over traffic, detouring the waiting time that wasn't demanded for the process. The traffic detoured also included individuals better suited for the task I was trusted with. The eagle is the Alpha of the air, yet his traveling ability is transitional. He's not wired to eternally fly which means at some points he needs rest too. It is interesting how when the eagle protected Israel from the Egyptians the eagle's battery of genetic strength never grew weary while on the job. It was Gods using natural to marshal protection for his own. A-Flat literally carried me to destinations that men including myself never would have never done.

A-Flat is a confidence for me that has proven to be strong enough to stand despite seasons of mild compliments and few applauses. Paul writes to the church at Philippi and states in chapter 1:6 that, *"Being confident of this, that he who began a good work in you will carry it on to completion until the day of Christ Jesus."* **Confidence** is a must but have it in God. I've seen that when it's in God, he then strengthens our self confidence in exchange. Overconfidence can be a combination of arrogance and or false narratives feeding a fantasy. However, there is a season that we can experience that perhaps individuals who once depended on you to make sure you had their approval can become offended because your confidence matured and no longer needs their endorsement. Not always, but these can often be the ones who label you as arrogant because your true shift from low self-esteem to confidence evicted the influence, they once had over you.

Every season for me was not an "Amen" season. Let me say this: *Every Amen won't come A Man or a Human.*

Theologically we find that 3 of the 27 New Testament books of the Bible according to the King James Version don't end in 'Amen': The book of Acts, James and John don't end with Amen as the other 24 do, yet they are and should be in the Bible. I want to push that every season won't be a season of affirmation by man. As we move forward to the next chapter let's remember that a private winner is greater than a popular but average personality.

In closing of this chapter gospel Phenom 'Sandra Crouch' the twin sister and musical accomplice of the legendary Andre Crouch wrote a song echoing Jesus from the Cross. She entitled it "MY GOD MY GOD, HOW EXCELLENT IS YOUR NAME".

May these lyrics bless you as they remind us that our mission was never intended for crowd examination but rather for the endurance of the cross....

My God, my God, my God

How excellence is your name

Glory honour to you we give

You're worthy of all our praise

All power all knowledge all wisdom

I fine in you

My saviour, Lord and king

How excellence is your name

My God, my God, my God

Holy holy and divine

Thou who reigns over all the earth

Fill my heart with peace

All power all knowledge all wisdom I fine any you

My saviour, Lord and king

How excellent is your name

Hallelujah hallelujah hallelujah hallelujah

Hallelujah hallelujah

How excellent is your name

Jesus, Your worthy of all my praise

My God, how excellent is your name i

Jesus your worthy of all our praise

My God, my God, my God

Source: Musixmatch

Songwriters: Sandra Crouch

CHAPTER 2

The Altar that Altered

In Genesis 22 Abraham's Altar of offering his son Isaac altered how I view God's provision. Abraham was laying out all he had to God and yet there was a ram in the bush, but only after God saw his heart. Many times, our lives are filled with transactions of "hellos and goodbye" and in true transparency that's not what bothers us most. The issue is when we have to say Goodbye before we have secured a new Hello (Selah). The new "Hello" wouldn't replace the grief of the goodbye but it would offer employment and resuscitation to damaged emotions saddened by the loss.

My son looked at me 5 years ago and said, "Dad, how do you feel not having ever being able to celebrate Mother's Day or Father's Day?" Externally I smiled while internally my heart slipped in a waterless sob. It reinforced to me that it was the Altar that had indeed Altered. I dug even deeper into my soul and discovered that both my triumphs and traumas were being released from the same well. I began to unravel what James the Apostles was speaking of in James 3:11(American Standard Version) when he interrogatively states *"Doth the fountain send forth from the same opening sweet water and bitter?"*

They shouldn't, but at times they do.

Might I also remind you that a 'well' has a location. In this case it was a location affectionately called "The Temple" though the official name was Miracle Temple Church of God In Christ, most referred to it with use of its affectionate name. It served as the state headquarters of the Kansas East Jurisdiction. It literally was a myriad of memories that was connected to me from that source. These memories collected a cadre of both Triumphs and Traumas.

Before I further expound, let's look and notate that the word trauma, is actually the Greek word for the word "wound" as in one that is wounded in the past, yet the trauma lives and lingers on. So, Miracle Temple is located at 2106 Quindaro Blvd. in Kansas City, Kansas. It was that place for me where Triumphs and Traumas collided.

Let's talk **triumphs**:

I sang in the States Shine Band earning an opportunity to play drums as a child. I was also allowed to test my up-and-coming skills as a beginner musician at age 12 playing for the State Youth Choir, who, at that time, was called the "Purity Class". I was able to become the state musician at age 14, training the choir, and teaching original music at age 20.

That was the location, then there's the Altar of the location. At the altar I was married to my wife of 22 years. I was licensed as a minister and later ordained as an Elder there. At that time, they had what was called the Radio Broadcast. I was able to preach on the broadcast at age 24. I had 11 minutes to preach with a 2-minute warning. I never forget getting up from the organ and jumping right into the sermon with a transition of only 30 feet in between. I was very blessed by The Temple and the faith. It really earmarked me for my calling as well as birthmarked me for who I am today.

Some of the trauma experienced at that same altar was my dad's funeral, as it was held there when I was only at the age of four. Sixteen years later, my mom's funeral was also held there.

Both of my maternal grandparents' homegoing's were there along with so many other retrospective traumas induced occurrences. I thought that the trauma would end there. It didn't.

Before I go further, I want to disclaim that this is a record of my story and testimony that I document to encourage someone. I also share this as a person that God healed from all of the wounds that at the time seemed unbearable, avoidable and unsolvable.

Let's continue... much of the trauma came from an experience of church hurt. I was looked over for a couple of positions on the state level that I desired at that time just because much of the work I was already doing. Some of this trauma by way of domino effect was self-induced, I just didn't know it at the time, but man enough to own. I had misdiagnosed the obligation of the church to me. In saying this I'm not being dismissive or shady at all, I really did misdiagnose it. Just because you may seemingly be the best fit does not mean you're automatically trusted to that position. Many other factors played a role, and the political role was just not my way, interest, or skillset. I did feel that if the fairness of egalitarianism was served out that things would go my way.

The question then becomes what do you do when your faithfulness works against you due to commonality? Well, my name wasn't called to be one the assistants to serve the state music department, neither did I ascend to the position of Pastor in my local church as it was also vacant at the time. Was I hurt? I was absolutely hurt. Some of the hurt I hid because it was avoidable, but I did learn from it. Before we address the hurt, I want to say three things.

First of three, I was honored to be considered as a 1 of the 4 candidates for my local church as well as being given an opportunity to interview for the pastorate role at the tender age of 27. It's a badge of grace to tell the whole story and not just how you are wronged. We all at times are the victims. However, it's never good to desire to be the victim.

Secondly, I'd say when hurt, don't applaud, or magnify the pain. Get the help needed and own where you're at mentally and emotionally and how you feel.

Thirdly, I'd say to the reader to know the difference between your Judas and your Peter. The Peter's will do you wrong due to a fleshly moment or human moment of erroneous judgment. Judas moves differently, he's wired to betray with no remorse. The pain from the two feels the same at the moment, but hot water cools down. So, Peter at the right time you **RESTORE**, but as for your Judas you **RELEASE**. The hurt I hid stemmed from the sacrifices I made that I didn't have to make, and neither was I asked to make. It was on me.

Here we go.

My wife and I lost our first child through an ectopic pregnancy the same week we were scheduled to attend a leadership conference for the denomination that we were a part of at the time. The hospital gave her a pill that would terminate the baby in the womb, and then pass through the stools. Knowing this was happening with her, we chose to attend the conference anyway; we were young and just trying to be faithful. The process of the pregnancy elimination occurred in our hotel room where the conference was held. This was devastating to me and my wife, however no one made us attend, it was a choice.

Then the other occasion was in the year 2000. We were married on Saturday March 11th. Two days later, on that Monday night guess where I am? I'm at the State Choir Rehearsal, again this was my choice. I loved what I did and did it with the right intention. However, I did feel that faithfulness would be closely looked at should opportunities present themselves.

Moving forward the lessons learned is that I would encourage anyone to draw boundaries with anyone and anything. Boundaries alone don't promote healing, but they do prevent much of the scabs, scars and splinters that occur when boundaries aren't established.

Let me say this another way: **Be very cautious of working on anything or for anyone with a "from can - to - can't" mindset**, because if and when it turns wrong it's usually a sharp turn. Working from "can to can't" is often accompanied with much mental drainage, physical setbacks, poor dieting, and increased hypertension.

This altar had altered me because the death of my parents and grandparents made me feel as if I had no voice. I was a nice person, so I was going to take it as I did, but also, I felt as if I had no inside man that was vouching for the protection of me. When I look back on not being selected for those appointments mentioned earlier, I learned that I had only lost politically but not spiritually, and that God's purposes were still at work in my life. The Altar of death did alter me because even had things went the way they did I could have reasoned with my parents for understanding, prayer and guidance on how to move on independent of the sting of bitterness.

his was jacked up, and I mean jacked up not having them around at this time, however I must admit that my relationship with God grew as a result of their absence. Through this I better comprehend what the prophet Isaiah was saying In Isaiah 6:1 (KJV) when he declared, *"In the year that king Uzziah died I also saw the Lord sitting upon a throne, high and lifted up, and his train filled the temple"*.

This is not unanimous but often people we love and that love us can sometimes prevent the relationship strength with Jehovah. It's not until their absence that we grow into a fuller and more intimate relationship with him. I currently have good relationships with all the people that are still alive that were involved during the affairs surrounding the hidden parts of my trauma that was explained. God can heal you!

The key of A-Flat is a particular pitch musically, but the **A** is only an alphabet. It stands for what you'd desire it to stand for. What I explained in this chapter may at times have left the feeling of ADVERSITY, as it was. Maybe I didn't get those APPOINTMENTS discussed, but it resolved in a greater ANOINTING for me.

The final thing about the altar that plagues, pinches, and at times pokes at my spirit is that I have no memory of my parents' final services. As briefly discussed in the Acknowledgments, I have obituaries but no real-time footage due to the pictures being misplaced as well as society during that time was not a social media era where you could use a cellphone to record the funeral services or stream and upload to YouTube and or Facebook. Though unfortunate and irrevocable, I will say that this dilemma allows me to remember them in Grace opposed to Grief. So, we must remember as discussed in Chapter One that the A-Flat minors though unpreferred are relatively a major in another key, so it's all a matter of perspective.

As we pivot into the next chapter, I'd love to leave you with the words of an old hymn of often sang in God's universal church entitled "SPIRIT OF THE LIVING GOD" composed by author, Daniel Iverson:

"Spirit of the living God,
Fall afresh on me.
Melt me, mold me, fill me, use me.
Spirit of the living God,
Fall afresh on me"

So, as he melts us, and molds, he's really ALTERING us and may use various Altars to accomplish it. Before what's Altered is a custom fit, its first measured then cut on. (SELAH)

CHAPTER 3

When Affirmation Announces Itself

(*Jesus being affirmed*) Matthew 3:16-17 recalls Jesus being Baptized and after he's baptized, he's then Affirmed. I was immensely intrigued by this because of how humble his beginnings were being homeless as well as the occupation of a nomadic carpenter. This further magnifies the idea of not to confuse your WHERE with your WHO. Where life currently finds you is not an accurate measure of who you really are. You can't think about it like that or accept such a jail sentencing label from people.

There were 3 observations in relation to the Affirmation of Christ that fuels the secret crush that I have with text. Here they are.

1.The Heavens Opened.

2. The Maker of Heaven Spoke Audibly

3. What Jesus Did to earn such affirmation

Okay, let's delve in and dissect these three observations....

The Heavens Opened

There are said to be 7 heavens, and since revelation is accumulative and conglomerative which means that by increment we discover the mysteries of God and the scriptures. The Apostle Paul said it another way in I Corinthians 13:9 (KJV), when he states that "*We know in part, and we prophesy in part.*" Though there are said to be 7 heavens we identify 3 of them universally. In Genesis 1:1 (KJV), He created the heaven (singular) and the earth. By Genesis 2:1 (KJV), The Heavens (plural) were complete.

- **First Heaven** - Most humans can see it. It's the atmospheric heavens where the birds fly, and airplanes travel. It's about 62 miles above earth according to NASA.
- **Second Heavens** are the celestial heavens where the astronauts travel, it's where the stars, sun, and moons and where the planets and galaxies are housed.
- **Third Heaven** is the dwelling place of God and the heavenly host.

So, when the heavens opened in Matthew, Chapter 3, it was the first New Testament mention of the **Open Heavens**. Who better to secure VIP seating for this thriller of an event conducted by the heavens than Yeshua, The Christ Man. I see the heavens as curtains on a stage. The curtain either allows and or disallows entry into the wealth share of God's divine economic system. The heavens are God's unlimited and unrestricted supply of storage bounty for all needed resources in the earth. So, when the Heavens opened for Christ, they also opened for us. After all we are according to Romans 8:17 (NIV), since we are children, then we are heirs of God and co-heirs with Christ. So those heaven are open waiting on our faith to access them.

One of favorite singers Tremaine Hawkins sang a popular gospel hit entitled "GOING UP YONDER " the song was phenomenal as was the response from the church in regard to the song. We also saw the word in scripture in Genesis 22:5 KJV where it states: *"And Abraham said unto his young men, Abide ye here with the ass; and I and the lad will go yonder and worship, and come again to you"*.

Again, *yonder* was associated with going up vertically. In this case it was Mount Moriah to experience worship for the time. I say the first time because this was a LAW OF MENTION, which means the first mention of a phrase or idea in scripture. Prior to this we don't see the word worship in the Bible, yet it was connected to some type of elevation of epic momentum and ecstatic climate referred to as yonder.

Well, this is good!

Additionally, though the Open Heavens loosened the belt a bit and allowed a more creative system that extended the warranty of grace, it also usurped impossibility with possible and unclogged the choke hold that religion had on God's elect.

How so Preacher?...

Well, because you don't have to die to access streets of gold as it enabled heaven on earth. Hebrews 11:13 BEREAN STUDY BIBLE, tell us, *"All these people died in faith, without having received the things they were promised. However, they saw them and welcomed them from afar. And they acknowledged that they were strangers and exiles on the earth."*

We live in a dispensation that allows us to experience manifestation upon demand by way of NOW FAITH!! This so amazing because it the holy writ demonstrates this so often for example in the KVJ:

- The phrase IT CAME TO PASS: shows up 727 times
- The word IMMEDIATELY, shows up in Mark's gospel 41 times,
- The word STRAIGHTWAY shows up 27 times,
- The word NOW shows up 621 times.
- The word SUDDENLY appears 87 times

This applauded the reality of Hebrews 4:12 where it says, *"For the word of God is quick, and powerful, and sharper than any two-edged sword, piercing even to the dividing asunder of soul and spirit, and of the joints and marrow, and is a discerner of the thoughts and intents of the heart."*

In 2007, there was a movie released called KNOCKED-UP, written, co-produced and directed by Judd Apatow, and starring Seth Rogen, Katherine Heigl, Paul Rudd, and Leslie Mann.

The summative theme of the movie was the repercussions of an intoxicated one-night stand between two strangers that resulted in an unintended pregnancy. In the visual concept it seemed to suggest that the intimacy shared was extremely brief, or what is cultural referred to as a QUICKIE (*watch me close*) ...

This MOTION PICTURE reminded me as I encourage you, the reader, that a *quickie* even though its quick, offers the same dividends as a longer session. In fact, it's more impressive due to getting the same gift quicker than those who rendered overtime. **HELLOOOOO** and Selah!!

The Maker of the Heavens spoke audibly

It was not only what was said, but also who said it. This was God who created all, knows all and sustains all. He made the announcement of affirmation for his son. I think it's best to learn to apply this, meaning that Jesus knew it was more appropriate to allow another to praise him as the Father did. God the father also knew that it was more appropriate to affirm his son because his son would lead peers who at times would struggle with his call. We have to allow God to do the affirming.

Proverbs 27:2 instructs the church to, "*Let another man praise you, and not your own mouth; A stranger, and not your own lips.*" If I was in a Pentecostal church and King Solomon were to read that and if we are honest, depending on who was there, in the midst of us would shout "PREACH SOLOMON" or "PREACHER YOU RIGHT" or, "SAY IT FOR THE PEOPLE IN THE BACK" (lol).

Ok let's move on fam....

In my journey there were times when I made the mistake of announcing too fast my next moves. We have to be honest, right, if we are to help someone else. That being said, when I would prematurely announce my next move, it was often to secure affirmation from my peers and upgrade my reputation. My announcements felt good coming from my mouth to their ears, but I lost power. I couldn't control what would be done with the information I shared. I gave them too much tea. So may I help somebody really quick… '*Don't give up the tea to orange juice minded people.*'

Sometimes my announcements created a stronger bond of support, while other times it created envy and competition. So, I'd almost never get the affirmation desired that way, rather I just had lost the piece of the friend that I thought I had.

I was often ahead of my time. The reason being that I feared being late for my time when that time came. It was at this point that I authentically understood King Solomon's word in Ecclesiastes 9:11c (KJV), when he stated, "*Time and Chance happeneth to them all*".

He was saying that we all get our time, we just have to first wait for it. Then upon its arrival steward it correctly by recognizing momentum and to work with it at that time. This is not to be confused with self-created momentum, as well as not allowing fear, distractions and bad decisions to sabotage it. Jesus allowed the Father to appoint him globally opposed to him forcing it with the return of a mere local reach. We also see the power of VOICE ACTIVATION here. It seemed to me that God himself obeyed Job 22: 28 (KJV) and made a decree. That decree was actually established simply because he spoke it which was a model of how we as Israel's remnants are to access our open heavens. Christ allowing God to Affirm was also necessary in that it preserved family relationships. Prior to Jesus coming was the mission, mandate and ministry of his cousin John the Baptist who had the lion's share of influence at that time. John was in tune with God but not necessarily Johns disciples. But when this

Announcement of Affirmation was made John and his following had heard it. This exonerated the pressure from Jesus to justify himself and who he was. We must know that why we are on God's agenda, that we are not the only one on his agenda. If we sit back and allow the Lord to advance us it detours much of the unnecessary drama, family conflict and offense that can come with God's vindication of us.

What did Jesus do to earn such affirmation?

Let me tell you what Jesus did to earn such affirmation he did simply NOTHING.

Let's follow the timeline grid of when God affirmed him. It was at the beginning of his public ministry which pre-dates even the first miracle at the wedding of Cana Galilee. He had not healed anyone, had not ran a revival, cleansed the leper, or even fed the 5000. He was affirmed for who he was. You have to know who you are. Resumes are necessary at times but at other times God will favor the fact that you're unlearned to magnify His glory and the brutal truth that He doesn't always call the qualified, but He often qualifies whom He has called. In fact, in the book of Acts 4:13 (KJV) says, "*Now when they saw the boldness of Peter and John, and perceived that they were unlearned and ignorant men, they marveled; and they took knowledge of them, that they had been with Jesus.*"

Excuse my transparency fam, but I'm not really sure that these disciples graduated high school, I'm just saying…. Ok, let's carry on church while pleading the 5th!

Furthermore, all David had going for him was 5 smooth stones and an extremely brief and weak resume. All the resume said, was that he killed a bear and a lion with his hands and that he tended to his father's sheep. Nothing more! Very unimpressive! Next applicant please! Sir we will call you if interested! You're short, we'd prefer taller! You're Too Young, we'd prefer older! You're too Heavy, we'd prefer healthier! Wrong gender, we'd prefer the other! Wrong race, we'd prefer a more diverse class! A 'was lost' until Goliath came and the earth by God's hand was ready to release to David what God had designed for him to have. Goliath was opposition for Israel but a mass opportunity for David. God knew it and David grew to understand it. As we attempt to put a bookmark in this chapter and prepare for the next. Please remember this: THOSE WHO MAN DON'T PREFER; GOD OFTEN CHOOSES TO PROMOTE.

Finally, there's a portion of lyrics to a song that I want to leave you with:

Because of who you are, I give you glory
Because of who you are, I give you praise
Because of who you are, I will lift my voice and say
Lord, I worship you because of who you are
Jehovah Jireh, my provider
Jehovah Nissi, Lord, you reign in victory
Jehovah Shalom, my Prince of Peace
And I worship you because of who you are

Source: LyricFind

Songwriters: Brian Kelly McKnight / Michael Brandon Barnes

God chooses us the same way he desires us to worship Him. Simply because of who He is, and because of who He made us to be.

CHAPTER 4

Accusations that Accompany Accomplishments

This chapter was shaped by a passage in Isaiah 59:19b (KJV) which states, *"When the enemy shall come in like a flood, the Spirit of the Lord shall lift up a standard against him."*

This text uses the word *flood*, which is much different from rain, mist, hail or snowstorm as survival can be attained by planting yourself in a safe area. The flood is a bit different as it forces a response of physical movement if drowning is to be avoided. It's important to differentiate the enemy of demonic influence that Isaiah is referring to apart from the natural consequences stimulated from poor decision-making.

There are **5** types of Enemies that I'd like to identify:

1. Enemies that struggle with your identity (Herod /Pharoah)

2. Enemies who are climbers – (Judas & Cain)

3. Enemies, who were first friends, but couldn't stomach the father's choice of you - (Joseph's brothers).

4. Enemies by default, out of an abundance of caution - (Abram/Lot)

5. The Enemy who's a *friend in person* but *an enemy in purpose* - (10 lepers)

Let's further examine:

1. ***Enemies that struggle with your identity*** hate your existence not because of who you are but of who you could become.

This is often a demonic spirit that troubles the one who afflicts the hate. We see this with King Herod and Pharaoh as both were willing to kill individuals that they didn't know just to engineer a genocide, in order to secure their seat of power. My advice is to avoid dealing with people who show signs of hating without a cause. Behind this spirit is often some type of prejudice and or bias that's played out through trivial pessimism.

2. *Enemies who are climbers*- Judas & Cain

Let's define "climbers". Climbers are people and systems whose uncontrolled ambition seeks to win and advance at any cost. Life confronts every human with such opportunities, however it's the climber who takes the bait, knowing the cost of winning may eliminate and or eternally bruise a relationship yet they proceed. These kinds really don't want to be your enemy, but they will never be a loyal friend either. They really desire for their climbing motivations to go unnoticed, and if noticed then they desire who they hurt to get over it without the graceful proof of demonstrated remorse. Climbers often are the ones who will first sin with you, and then eventually sin against you. *Selah.* The most brutal lesson here is that we choose them and allow them access. We didn't know it at the time, but we chose them. Jesus even admits this in John 13:18 (NIV).

The solution here is simply to "Travel Light". Make people earn you. Not because of you but to make certain that they can respect your life's calling and journey. This will then allow you to determine what level of access for you to assign them. Judas loved Jesus but not greater than his climbing spirit. But Judas illustrates to us that climbers often hang themselves as he did. Cain the brother of Abel killed him, not because he hated him but rather the cruel spirit of jealousy was at work.

3. *Then there are those who can only befriend you as long as they can keep up with you*- However, if they feel that you've surpassed them, then there's your problem. I've learned that it's possible to *go* together but not *grow* together. This creates an unequally yoked partnership no matter the origin of the relationship. Joseph's brothers were fine with him until he received a badge of honor in the form of a coat that recognized the favor upon his life. In Genesis 37:3-4 it tells us that the coat was kaleidoscoped with colors, suggesting a public seat to the Lord's table of his choicest and most trusted servants. I want to go on record saying that the coat didn't cause the hate but rather exposed it. Likewise, many of you are in your season of the Joseph Anointing. I say this in the sense of being selected as the chosen from among the many called as stated in Matthew 22:13.

Remember though, while Joseph reigned with God and for him, it was not independent of a struggle. So, I encourage you to stay committed even during the phases of processing. Just as God allowed him to be sold into slavery, be reminded that he was sold and bought, not given away and spoiled. Even the enemy knows your worth and at times helps us to further discover it by hating you on levels that you didn't know we were on.

4.Enemies by default out of an abundance of caution- Abram & Lot. Abram and Lot never had a problem that we read about; it was simply the herdsmen that were beefing with each other that ultimately caused their separation. Haran who was a biological brother of Abram had a son named Lot. Haran then dies and Abram takes Lot, his nephew in as his own. While this was noble, I want to reinforce to you the reader that: **Everyone is not your assignment**.

Then there are some that are your assignment by way of a DIVINE LEASE AGREEMENT in other words they are *seasonal*.

- Some fruits are only ripe: when in season
- Some vegetables are only nutritional: when in season

- Some clothes are only worn effectively: when season
- Some prayers can only be answered when in season. Enemies can be formed when we don't consider seasons.

Notice the voyage of Abram. He traveled 700 miles to Iraq, then another 700 miles into Syria, another 800 down to Egypt, and then back to Israel. This was impressive to me because he traveled 22,000 miles to be in the will of God. Lot, on the other hand was on the journey as a visitor who was blessed by association. I believe that Abram grew to understand that "SEPARATION WAS NOT TERMINATION". Separation was simply being "set apart", and that there are times when God has to Decommission your circle to Rightfully Commission your paths. It doesn't terminate the relationship; it just adds balance by way of boundaries to it.

5. *The Enemy Who's A friend in Person but an Enemy in Purpose.* I've learned that some people will follow you to your grave and so often those same people will help aid you in getting to your grave without purpose being complete. I often instruct those I mentor to never go low places for company. It's better to eat alone when you know what you bring to the table. This final type of enemy is really never an enemy to the person, just an enemy to the purpose. The 10 lepers in Luke 17 were friends as we see they traveled in packs enabling each other. However, the day came when separation had to happen. One wanted more and gave more. He offered gratitude for what God had done and was granted wholeness while the remaining 9 were only gifted healing. The difference being that the healing cured the spotted skin while wholeness cleansed a spotted spirit.

Enemies to purpose usually are not long distance but rather close in the proximity of an arm's reach. They can be spouses, best friends, lovers, baes, and boo thangs.

Accomplishments seem to have a fatal attraction with accusations...

Revelation 12:10b (NKJV) says, *"For the accuser of our brothers and sisters, who accuses them before our God, day and night, has been hurled down."*

The assumption here is that accusations may have had an impact at the time, but over time they are weapons that simply won't prosper. As tough as it appears, sometimes giving attention to accusation and trying to justify yourself becomes the quicksand in which people hemorrhage up on. We have to continue to be the remnant as we saw Peter, James, and John in the inner circle of Christ. But then we also have to be the rare remnant as we saw Peter who stood out from among these three. But remember child of God, it was when he looked at his circumstance while walking on water that Peter began to sink.

Don't worry about your accuser, they will come to reap what they've sown. In fact, they are on God's hate list in relation to behaviors. Proverbs 6:16 reminds us, *"...the six things doth the Lord hate, yea, seven are an abomination unto him: [17]A proud look, a lying tongue, and hands that shed innocent blood, [18]An heart that deviseth wicked imaginations, feet that be swift in running to mischief, [19]A false witness that speaketh lies, and he that soweth discord among brethren."* As we transition into the next chapter, I want to leave some lyrics to a song with you written by Fred Hammond & Radical For Christ entitled "No Weapon":

God will do what he said he would do
He's not a man that he should lie (stand by his word) he will
come through
Oh, I won't be afraid of the arrow by day
From the hand of my enemy
I can stand my ground with the Lord on my side
For the snares they have set will not succeed.
No weapon formed against me shall prosper
It won't work.

Finally, I want to say that I strongly believe that God often allows accusations because in some weird way it's connected to advertisement. Could it be that he uses the channel of the accusations to prepare that table before us in the presence of our enemies, the accuser? I think so! Keep Accomplishing... You will overcome and outlive the accusations.

CHAPTER 5

Apostolic Addresses

In this chapter it's my desire to expound upon the parity of locale and humans used by God to accomplish his will in and through us.

Let's first examine Ephesians 4:11 (KJV) where is declares: *And he gave some, apostles; and some, prophets; and some, evangelists; and some, pastors, and teachers.*

Before getting into apostolic addresses let's gain more of an acquaintance with the nature of the Apostolic function. The Apostle is more managerial than the other graces. For some, I remind, and to others I inform in a format of brevity in relation to the job description of the five graces. I will use the human hand as reference points of mental visuals of what's best known as THE FIVE-FOLD ministry.

So, the **Prophet** guides the sheep, referenced as the index finger for pointing. The **Evangelist** gathers the sheep as referenced with the middle finger which is the center point of the hand and tallest of them signifying optimized frequency and balance. The **Pastor** guards the sheep as a watchman represented with a ring finger suggesting the therapeutic marriage he or she has with the sheep. Then there's the **Teacher** who grounds the sheep as seen with the pinky finger suggesting there is so little of it when compared to the need for it.

Finally, but also biblically enlisted first was the **Apostle,** who governs. The word govern can translate to mean government which is a managerial term of operation. Obviously on the hand it is the thumb, as the thumb is the only hand limb that can touch the face of all other finger limbs. The Apostle in its truest form is one who at times functions in all the other graces mentioned in Ephesians 4:11.

Over the past couple of years, I've noticed an uptick in how certain locations are assigned to certain ministry gifts. Sometimes these locations are church residences and can be secular organizations used by God as his hand of provision. This can be a doozy because they can change as it did with Elijah in First Kings 17 when God reassigned his Domain of influence. The brook of Cherith had sustained by way of stream and the ravens who brought him bread and protein twice daily. This was a miracle within itself because ravens will kill their own if they don't leave them first. Their season did well but had run its course. The brook had dried up just as the ravens had begun to die off, but God through this changed his APOSTOLIC ADDRESS. He was appointed to Zarephath where the DESTINY LINK of a nameless widow had sustained him. This can also be referred to as a "Prophetic Zip Code". When destiny links meet all parties win. In the widow's case she had a meal, but it lacked capacity while the prophet had the power to command capacity pulling it from little. Baking her last cake for the prophet before death actually became her last day of poverty before life in fullness began. They both won!

Your Vicinity must be revisited because it can change

Your calling can also change and so it must be revisited annually with prayer as well. The questions I'd admonish you to ask yourself is *where am I assigned to serve?* Though we are called to give ourselves away, where is your refueling station? Where has God often favored you? Of course, we know God is omnipresent and can operate kingdom purposes independent of locale, but where is the territory that the blessings of God are most bountiful?

Apostolic Addresses/ Prophetic Zip codes used in the Bible
River Chebar-

In Ezekiel 1:1 the heavens opened up while at this river. This same river was mentioned eight times in his book as a frequency of residential stability. This was an Apostolic Address for him. It was a place of comfort, life, and manifestation. How lucky is the prophet to have the heavens open as a token of God's affirmation in the very verse. I believe this can and will be you. It was also a vicissitude of irregularity to see that in Ezekiel 1:3 how the word of the Lord came to Ezekiel expressly as in like first class mail out on a rush order. Yes, without delay! CHEBAR means strength and or force. It seems to me that this river was an assigned territory and as long as he was committed to where he was assigned, he would prosper as he did.

River Gihon-

Another was *River Gihon: Genesis 2:13, it means to "Burst forth", but it was also where kings were appointed. Solomon was told by his dying father King David to meet him at this river in 1 Kings 1:33. David anointed him and crowned him king despite David's other son who was older and had attempted to self-appoint himself as king. May I encourage you to find that secret place, posture and or piety that will reignite your expectation and discernment to know where God has you. May you blossom where you've been planted.

Tigris/Hiddekel-

In Genesis 2:14, Tigris/Hiddekel means "Swift Current". It's a tributary that fed into the Euphrates River which means that this was a place of overflow. I feel the urge to prophesy that your next is here and that it's going be so abundant that you will become a tributary to others just as this river did.

In fact, in Daniel 10:4, it served as the river of Spiritual Insight & Angelic Appearances as Daniel heard the words of the God through the angel. Look at these Apostolic Addresses and how they matter. Oh snaps, I can't forget my favorite one which was the: Jordan River:

Jordan River-

I love this one because 2Kings, Chapter 2 demonstrates how generational mantles were transferred here. Hold on church not only that but Jesus was also baptized there, there as the heavens opened up there.

The same can be said for Obed Edom the gentile who had three free exclusive months with the access of the ark. 2 Samuel 6:11 (NKJV) tells us, *"The ark of the LORD remained in the house of Obed-Edom the Gittite for three months, and the LORD blessed him and his entire household."* This was a prophetic Zip for David. Once he knew it was still at work without his presence he went back and retrieved it. This also reveals that God's glory was not dependent on man and would shine regardless. As David did, sometimes we have to go back and revisit what, where and even who we took for granted (now that will preach).

Destiny Links

Apart from the Apostolic Addresses there at times can be a person whom God sends specifically for you. I call them "DESTINY LINKS" used by God to affirm, connect, unlock, confirm and or prepare with insight the needed revelation for your assignment. Destiny Links are like some links to a computer meaning that can expire if there is a distraction that prevents hearing the word of the Lord. Destiny Links are often time capsules ready to release at certain times.

Destiny Links can be friendly, but in most cases aren't called to be friends, that is not their assignment!

In Samuel 16, the prophet Samuel was a destiny link for David anointing him the first time of three. This put him in the company of King Saul. Then King Saul became a Destiny Link for David as he put him in the hearts of Israel, but that link would soon expire. Saul who promoted him one week was trying to kill him the next. I use this analogy to enforce the importance of not becoming so common with the destiny link that you lose your influence and ability to pivot when necessary.

Many of you perhaps may have made the mistake of becoming a best friend with a destiny link which can negate what God purposed them for. Many times, they were sent for a reason, not a season and definitely not a lifetime. My advice to someone who may have made this mistake is to simply take it as education, learning from it. Your next Destiny link is soon to come, in fact it's already been shipped.

I remember a time when God used a friend of mine to become a destiny link for me, opening up the door for me to present original music on an international level. He was an awesome songwriter and prolific musician himself. Pastor Keith Newton of Kansas City was his name. I was literally down to nothing after just burying my mother six months prior. While in Kansas City, he said to me it would be nice if you would consider teaching your song to the national choir for what was then called "Song Is Born". I told him that I was going to try to make it happen to at least get there unbeknownst to me that he would utilize his connections the way he did.

He speaks in very calm manner, but he plays music very skillfully enthusiastically. He said to me after I had gotten to the convention, "Mike I'm gonna see if I can talk to Professor Iris Stevenson (who was International Music Department Leader at the time) to see if I can get them to give you a few minutes to teach your song, 'Blessed Be The Name Of The Lord' ". What he did not know is that before the afternoon rehearsal that very day I had just learned that my rented car had been towed and that my motel had been broken into. When I tell you that I barely and I mean barely went to the rehearsal, but I'm glad I did. Walking to the convention center into the rehearsal Keith Newton was walking around the halls trying to find me. We connected and he stated, "Mike I talked to the assistants to Professor Stevenson." These assistants by the way at the time were the late Deacon Kelvin Lennox and Evangelist Dorinda Clark Cole". He continues, "they said they should be able to squeeze you into a ten-minute gap.

I was floored as my name was eventually called... I started teaching the song from the organ with Emanuel Newton from Kansas City on the drums. After the choir kind of got it at the six-minute mark, I surrendered the organ to Keith and went to the stage. The rest was history, especially after the song modulated keys and made it to the key of A-Flat (hello).

A few lessons here that I want to dig into

1. I had to show up despite feeling jacked up. If I don't show up it never happens.
2. Though I was gifted I had to also operate in the same graceful character that Keith Newton was known for. It does matter, it can't only matter when his recommendation opens the door. I've got to live up to the same spiritual grace that he was known by.

3. Life often messes you greatly in the same season that it blesses you greatly! Hang on and stay with God.

4. I would go on to train the international music department in my original compositions for four years in a row off of that open door of a destiny link. They all began to know me on a first name basis because of availability and character that was connected with the gift.

5. There were others who could have helped me get on who didn't but when God is favoring you it's not your assignment neither is it necessary to speak out at those who could have helped but didn't. Just show up and properly steward the door that's been opened and honor the Lord for opening it.

Destiny links come in the most obscure packages, in the most peculiar forms and from the most sometimes unlikely people. So, make certain that all people are treated with respect. Never think just because you don't need someone today that you won't tomorrow.

Let's talk personally....

On April 19th, 2021, I was presented the opportunity to preach on PTWWN, Preach The Word Worldwide Network. This was my first time there. That day I engaged in an interview and afterward proclaimed the preached Word of The Lord. Later that afternoon I was the musical guest for the show America's Got Anointing. Both ministry opportunities were on the same network. The night before I was one of the music guests at Atlanta Live TV. It was a ball as I had no issues or complaints at all, but I knew the relationship with PTWWN would grow.

Two months later I was invited back that June to PTWWN, but this time I became family and appeared so many times afterwards that I've lost count. That network had become a

Apostolic Address for me. The relationship was never forced but rather scheduled by the Lord. This speaks to locale.

Let's now deal with the Destiny Link. The CEO of the network is, her Grace Apostle Marilyn Todman. She became my spiritual mother as I love her and Bishop Todman dearly.

True Story

I was doing a TV taping at the beautiful PTWWN studios in May of 2022. Around noon we grabbed a bite to eat. Afterwards, Apostle Todman invites me to sit in on a meeting about becoming an author. This meeting was scheduled for 2:00pm. It was at this meeting I then met Dr Ellison who presented those of us in the room with the information about publishing and becoming an author. I later discovered that his wife had suffered a stroke and due to this unfortunate circumstance, he almost canceled. Listen fam, had he canceled the meeting and with my flight departure back to Kansas City, four hours later, it would have prevented me from meeting him and connecting with the publishing company. That said, there were two destiny links at work here while simultaneously connected to the Apostolic Address of PTWWN. Had Dr. Marilyn Todman not invited me to the show then I would've never met Dr. Ellison who presented the Publishing deal with Leeds Press for this very book you are reading.

The Point: God has a way linking the right people at the right time. I share this to remind you that God has resources everywhere. He knows how to release his supernatural wind to blow whatever to you that he wants you to have when he wants you to have it!

There's one more spin to this story. I had an opportunity to go and do a small tour with the Prince of Gospel, John P. Kee. It was literally down to one final confirming call that I never received. A local Bishop in my area of Kansas City personally knew John P. Kee and had called him on my behalf as well as recommending me and connecting all the dots in my interest. In a sense of transparency, the truth is, had I got the confirming call I would have gone. When I look back on it, especially the schedules, I would not have been able to be a part of that tapping at "Preach the Word Worldwide Network" that May of 2022. This also would have forfeited me connecting with Leeds Press and signing the publishing contract. I am so grateful that the Bishop and great friend of mine, Apostle Larry B. Aiken of Kansas City was so willing to call on my behalf vouching for me. It reminded me there are still some good people in high places and are willing to pay it forward.

God knows all things and creates scenarios to perfection. Life in the Key of A-Flat also teaches that every opportunity may not be for you. Just because you can and may desire too doesn't mean it's for you. In life the best person doesn't always get the job, the right person does.

Apostolic Addresses, Prophetic Zip Codes and Destiny Links are beyond phenomenal because they are God-sent, spiritually endowed, and infused to serve Kingdoms purposes on earth. However, it does not release the human from responsibility.

Do I speak of prayer? Yes of course, but not so fast! Might I also totally defend prayer's purpose as it does work. I compare it to chocolate chips. Chocolate chip cookies cannot happen without the chocolate chips, but also chocolate chip cookies can't happen with only chocolate chips. This is likened to prayer. You will never get where you're going in God without prayer. Additionally, though you will never get where you're going if all you did was pray and never made moves. Have we forgotten what the Bible says.

Let's read it….

James 2:14 NLT says, "What good is it, dear brothers and sisters, if you say you have faith but don't show it by your actions? Can that kind of faith save anyone?" As we dim the light on this chapter preparing the props for the next let reinforce some A-Flat realities. The A-Flat mentality plugged me into many opportunities and on many stages. Some that were even unwelcoming but because I was needed, I was tolerated. Some of the people that God used to create platforms for me in various ways were people that didn't know that I knew I wasn't their first choice. My assignment was not to correct them or to prove to them why I should have been considered first. It was simply to see God as the loyal source who had never forgotten about me. (Praise Break).

Living Life in the Key of A-Flat is also knowing how to ignore the noise, find peace, count your blessings, preserve your positive energy and to understand that sometimes your plan B was God's plan A. Also, you do well to note that there will be people that call upon you for opportunities only because who they preferred was unavailable. They were still being used by God to favor you. You might have been their last choice but still God's first choice as He knew it and orchestrated it.

Before our time in chapter 5 time expires. I'd like to share a portion of lyrics to a song that I feel is befitting by Brian Courtney Wilson entitled: "Worth Fighting For"

Eyes haven't seen
Ears haven't heard
All You have planned for me
And nothing can separate me from Your love
When there's so much more
Still worth fighting for.
Source: Musixmatch
Songwriters

Fight the right battles the right way. Don't expend hours of energy for senseless causes. As we have discussed Apostolic Addresses and the importance of knowing your appointed territory, I urge you all to continue to ascend abundantly where you've been assigned.

CHAPTER 6

Amos the Prophet becomes an Ally

Wow! We've made it to chapter 6 and I'm elephant excited and alligator anxious to unpack my heart's sentiments with you.

Since I've kept it a buck with you this far, please allow me to continue with transparency. This chapter title revolves around the piercing reality that there was a time that I felt not being a (PK), Preacher's Kid had shut me out of opportunity considerations. While my view on it has changed, my observations at the time were a real thing. It wasn't until my last semester prior to graduating with my bachelor's degree from MidAmerica Nazarene University that there was a shift in my perspective. This evolution was heralded by a scripture in the book of Amos the minor prophet. At the time I was enrolled in an Old Testament Class with emphasis on the books of prophets. It was then that I bumped into a passage in Amos that appetized my curiosity and expanded my consciousness theologically. Prior to in depth studies scholastically I always thought of cookies when I thought of Amos. You all remember that brand called "Famous Amos Cookies"?

The scripture that captured my affections was found Amos 7: 14-15 KJV, *"Then answered Amos, and said to Amaziah, I was no prophet, neither was I a prophet's son; but I was an herdman, and a gatherer of sycamore fruit: 15And the Lord took me as I followed the flock, and the Lord said unto me, Go, prophesy unto my people Israel."*

This passage resonated with me because Amos wasn't biologically connected to a dynasty, yet God used him. Neither was he a prophet, which suggests he wasn't given a title before payment, yet he ascended (Selah). I've paid off a few cars in my life and was given the title independent of a lien only after all payments were made. I want to say that God can be in a dynasty as he was at certain times in the Bible. All dynasties are not demonic and or self-appointed by fleshly intellect. Then there are situations of nepotism that can creep into the body of Christ causing alienation to the point of identity crisis for some and then spirit displacement for others.

In my days of theological academia, I learned that Amos was 3rd in succession of the 12 minor prophets and according to the Hebrew Bible his name means " To Carry/Bourne Of God" which caused me to view him as an Old Testament type and shadow of Christ. One despised and rejected men. One who is called to do extraordinary things but from a vocation of simplicity such as a Herdsmen as Amos was.

This chapter has slippery slope tendencies because while I desire to encourage all who perhaps aren't (Preachers Kids) it wouldn't be at the expense of Preacher Kids. In Fact, I'd like to clarify that my son is PK as well as many of my close friends. Receiving whatever they received was not the problem, it was just often a muted voice of justice concerning those who weren't one per my experience. I like many of you were among the overlooked because of something I couldn't control. That was what created an issue for me. I remember departing a denomination in large part because after running a silent and personal diagnostic test by way of observation on the distribution of power. My view for the most part was that the majority who were deemed as dignitaries were connected to a dynasty or were given assignments because of mutable and or beta personalities. My pondering question was this, was there room for the diplomatic alpha who just wanted to serve. I may have graded this wrong analytically, but I resolved that at the time that there wasn't room. I also would share that part of this decision was that other reformations that hadn't known me or birthed me opened their arms, trust, and budgets to me. So it was the combination of those hybrid activities that landed me into a season of departure.

Here's my stance, if you are not a Pk, if you're not a brown noser, or a shrewd politician please know that God has designated a detour for you and that you will get to your winning season. On the contrary, if you are a PK and God has blessed and entrusted you with favor, please continue to do God's work in integrity as my love, high hopes and prayers are with you. We win together!

With the high hope of reviving someone else's spirits. I want to share a bit reflectively about Divine Detours and how God has a way utilizing his detour clause in the kingdom to whom he will according to his pleasure. In November 2016, one of my favorite preachers Bishop George Bloomer was in town. Along with several awesome qualities he possesses, the resounding thing that I love about him was how authoritative he is theologically in the Word. The host pastor for this event was the honorable Bishop Mark C. Tolbert of Kansas City.

I enjoyed the word and worshiped immensely that night. At the conclusion of worship, I wanted to speak to the visiting Bishop as the line was extremely long. I was tired and hungry, so I gave up on speaking to Bishop Bloomer. Upon my departure from the sanctuary, I heard a loud voice shouting my last name PORTLEY! PORTLEY! It was Bishop Mark Tolbert telling me in a very kind but urgent way for me to give him my CD so he could give it to George Bloomer. I went to my truck and got a few of them as the line started to drastically decrease. A few moments later Bishop Tolbert discussed with Bishop George Bloomer about me being a musical guest on the "Preach the Word" show on the Word Network. I couldn't believe this was happening and even with such a promising conversation there's still that silent question of would they call me back and confirm. Well, they did. The point here that I really want to drive is that God has resources everywhere and in just living day-to-day life and showing up for your responsibilities with the right attitude gives God so much to work with. Two months later from their conversation I made my appearance on the Word Network. Yes, me, the one who was not the son of a prophet just as Amos wasn't had been looked at by God. This is very important to magnify that originally, I went to the worship service to support and in supporting a door international door opened for me.

"Support Is Often a Frequent Ingredient To Success"

I learned something about myself with this opportunity because you think you know yourself, until you meet pressure. Listen children, let's walk this out. Pressure brings to surface not who you desire to be or portray to be but who you really are. 45 minutes before I'm scheduled to sing on the Word Network, they tell me that it's not just a taping but that we would be live in real time. This really changed the dynamic and heightened the risk because any mistake made could not be recalled.

What I learned is that it really didn't bother me. It was as if the situation had exposed me to me. Silently ever since then I knew that my ministry had a relationship with TV and that the time would come when opportunity would meet preparation.

Amos's ministry was an ally to my view because I identify with his process. I make the final motion that ultimately God is the greatest ally that we have and will ever need. Hallelujah!

Then there was another situation that I feel led to share as I was preparing for my Live Recording in 2014 and was hospitalized 2 weeks prior because of worry. I was worried about the budget to a point that my blood pressure resembled stroke level numbers. I had asked my uncle in the person of the late Bishop Ervin Sims, a phenomenal man, to expedite the offertory that evening. There simply was no one else more capable hands down than him. My worry that agitated me was if my city would show up.

The city showed up as we had about 1000 in attendance. However prior though each of the 6 musicians contracted were to receive $500 upon their completion of the night. Might I also add that they were very generous to charge such a competitive price when graded by the large body of material that they had to learn and produce in one setting. This was a chunk of change for me. At the time I was paid monthly by my secular employer, so I saved my check thinking if all goes wrong then I'll pay them from this. That would've covered that night, but I still would have had to pray for gas, utilities, and necessities the next week... (Hello somebody). The Lord showed me something that night by using the gift and grace of Bishop Ervin Sims Jr. as he simply talked to the people, made known the need and created an integral giving culture. When I tell you that we exceeded the need with one appeal, we did just that. The lesson I was supposed to learn is that you can't be God giving, you can't beat him thinking you can't beat him strategizing so stop worrying and put it all in his hands.

Many of you may be like me as was the prophet Amos and maybe you feel some sense of defeat because your grandfather wasn't the chief apostle, your grandmother wasn't the 'queen' over everything, or uncle the Baptist moderator or you're the brother, a cardinal to the Pope. Perhaps you don't come from much. All God needs from you is total submission to him and watch him begin to work the miraculous in your life. I speak this scripture over you. Let's declare it;

Matthew 20:16 (KJV)- " *So the last shall be first, and the first last: for many be called, but few chosen.*"

This same prophet prophesies to Israel some words that I want to speak over you as well from Amos 9:13-15 (Message)

"*Yes indeed, it won't be long now.*" God's Decree.

"*Things are going to happen so fast your head will swim, one thing fast on the heels of the other. You won't be able to keep up. Everything will be happening at once—and everywhere you look, blessings! Blessings like wine pouring off the mountains and hills. I'll make everything right again for my people Israel*" Amen!

One thing that I've learned about God is that he has a memory and takes notes! Well, remember Amos was a minor profit along with 11 of his contemporaries. They are only referred to as minor prophets because of quantity contribution but never because of their quality or importance. So much like Amos there were 2 other minor prophets named Zechariah and Hosea. These two minor prophets both have books each containing 14 chapters.

It was interesting to me that these two prophets have 14 chapters in volume yet are minor, while Daniel has 12 chapters in volume, but he's considered a major prophet. The spirit spoke to me about a year ago and told me to begin to proclaim and declare that the season of Zechariah and Hosea are upon us.

Zechariah's name means in Hebrew "Yahweh Remembers" while Hosea's name means "Salvation" signifying a mass deliverance. Many of you are like Hosea and Zechariah as in you're doing major things but getting minor results in exchange.

The Lord says to you through me that your days of sowing a whirlwind type of seed but getting only a fruit ripple in return are over. Your days of laborious toil with minor manifestations are over. In fact, in the very near future the bounty and blessings of God will begin to overtake you. Much of this is from previous prayers prayed, previous seeds sown and even trials endured. Hosea and Zechariah are speaking to us saying, *Welcome and congratulations on your new season where God has remembered and will deliver.* Hallelujah! Thank You Jesus!

While releasing this word to you, I must caution you to not make the modern-day Daniels your focus or your problem. Our assignment is not to be the opposition of those who have the favor of God upon their life. Daniel being a major prophet was God's call. Often when we as humans are handled with injustice, we subconsciously make accusations against those whom God has his hand on. They are not your problem. God doesn't have to cancel anyone out to promote you. He has cattle on a thousand hills.

Psalm 50:10 (NIV), "*For every animal of the forest is mine, and the cattle on a thousand hills. I know every bird in the mountains, and the creatures of the field are mine. If I were hungry, I would not tell you, for the world is mine, and all that is in it.*

We must understand that advancing together and not at the expense of one another is God's way.

Stay out of the quicksand of turning a cold spirit against people who others compete and compare you with. The tendency is to defame them which is beneath and unbecoming of who God has called you to be. God can pull you up without pulling them down.

Amos' name again means "Bourne of God". This word borne from an etymology mindset suggests to me to be something transported by air, by spirit and or by weight. Amos becomes an ally because he was built to last and not build to break as you were. Your trouble won't last always and though it overstays without permission and or invitation you will outlive it. You were born to win because you were borne to carry.

Remember Amos was a herdsman. A herdsman by definition is the owner or keeper of a herd of domesticated animals. This means that he was often at risk of getting bit the those he was caring for. Nothing can cause bitterness like a bite from someone you would bite others to protect. Amos as a herdsman was trained to train. He trained the animal's temperamental control. Many of those we are called to serve come to us without having the acquired skill set of temperamental control. As a cycle people often kill what's uncontrollable, signifying the death of relationships.

I think it necessary to understand why the biting occurs. Some people bite because of fear of being bitten first. Some bite because that was all they were modeled. Then some bites occur because God allowed it to birth a forgiving spirit in us. The levels that I believe God has for you are so high that it will require you to shake some bites off as Paul did in Acts 28 5-6 (NIV):

5But Paul shook the snake off into the fire and suffered no ill effects. 6 The people expected him to swell up or suddenly fall dead;

but after waiting a long time and seeing nothing unusual happened to him, they changed their minds and said he was a god.

Not only did he shake it off, but the fact he could withstand it proved his character to the barbarians who prior to the bite were suspicious about him. We actually don't read where Paul killed the viper or Amos the animals. Some people like Paul you shake off and survive. As for Amos some animal acting people you're called to shake off then pick back up to train while loving them. *(Ouch! That part! You sure preacher?!)*

Amos, to me, was literally the salt of the earth as stated in Matthew 5:13a(NIV) *"You are the salt of the earth. But if the salt loses its saltiness, how can it be made salty again?"*

I say this because salt is a condiment that in most cases you can't see in the food but can taste. Also, it is food that you don't necessarily smell as an advertising signal, yet you still taste. You can see cheese, pork chops or fruit but for the most part not salt. We have to be okay with not being overpromising and un-delivering. Also, Amos teaches us to totally let God elevate us because when his enemy the priest Amaziah attacked him in Chapter 7, misrepresenting his intentions to King Jeroboam God protected him. Many times, God didn't protect some because he never orchestrated the elevation. Taking pictures with celebrities for likes and momentum has its place, but that alone won't get you there. Supporting behaviors that you know God frowns upon and or rubbing elbows with those of a pedigree you desire alone won't do it. Stay with God and trust his timing.

Life in the Key of A-Flat life at times found its identity likened to drinking a "Diet Coke" after going to McDonald's ordering and eating a double quarter pounder sandwich with cheese, large fries, apple pie, and a baker's dozen of cookies. It was a placebo. Just as the diet coke could not seal the meal in healthy nutrition neither did A-flat fix any of my many issues; but because it was a therapeutic placebo, that was my way. My fix harnessed from A-flat in low moments was more hopeful than actual. It was also a placement factor. Just as the Diet Coke was ordered last but drank throughout the meal in most cases, so it was with my nerves at the climax of tough days on my piano.

As we conclude this segment I want to conclude in light humor. There was once a joke that was reality for me. It states that …'All my real old school worshipers will understand this' then shares this acronym

IDKWYCTDBICTCMH!

That meant: "I Don't know what you come to do but I come to clap my hands'"

Author- Unknown.

When this verse was sung in my faith circle, guess what key it was usually in? Answer: **A-Flat**

Just as we praised our way through our persecutions, our pressures, and our pain we are going to now praise our way out of Chapter 6 into Chapter 7.

CHAPTER 7

The Anointing: Its use and its abuse

In this chapter I hope to defend the anointing effectively without diminishing or over analyzing it. Let's go....

The word "anointing" according to the Oxford Languages Dictionary means to smear or rub with oil, typically as part of a religious ceremony. By permission of the Holy Spirit, I would also say it is a divine imprint legitimizing Kingdom approval that subdues demonic attacks as well as empowers and enforces the principles of God naturally, supernaturally, and lawfully in the earth. In depth studies tell us that there were 3 major parts to the temple of Jerusalem.

- The outer court was the first part as it represented the gift.
- Then the inner court was the second part as it is represented by the anointing.
- The last part was referred to as the most holy place representing the glory of God.

Our gift is a picture of the human's total capacity in our genetic innate ability to play out who we are by what we do in relation to passion and purpose. Our anointing is our gift submitted to God and his breath upon it as his sign of approval. This was seen in John 20:22 (NIV)-"And with that he breathed on them and said, "Receive the Holy Spirit."

The glory is the sum total attributes of God that's often atmospheric at times but also reflective in our lives as proof of its abode in us. The Greek word for "glory" is the word "Doxa" where we pull the English word doxology. A doxology was the final prayer prayed in some of the epistles as well as a song sung in many reformations to conclude the worship experience. Come on y'all don't get deep on me. Some of y'all remember that song sang to worship:

Praise God, from whom all blessings flow;

Praise Him, all creatures here below;

Praise Him above, ye heav'nly host;

Praise Father, Son, and Holy Ghost!

(*Written Thomas Ken in year 1674)

It was likened to the end, such as the OMEGA, the final letter of the Greek alphabet. We know that God has no end as his mercy endureth forever and his birth and seemingly death dates are from Everlasting to Everlasting. "Thank You God for Jesus" because he never dies! Well while the glory is the highest attribute of God as it's his combined essence in a unified manner, there are different manners of his glory. The Apostle states it this way in 2 Corinthians 3:18 (ESV), "And we all, with unveiled face, beholding the glory of the Lord, are being transformed into the same image from one degree of glory to another. For this comes from the Lord who is the Spirit."

There's often a misunderstanding of the glory of God apart from the anointing. The key difference is that the anointing needs the human for it to live whereas the glory needs the flesh to die for it to live. (Selah)

The anointing electrifies as a surge through a person, but the glory electrocutes. This is often seen in both the loss of physical senses and intended order worship as it was with 2 Chronicles 5:14 (KJV), "So that the priests could not stand to minister by reason of the cloud: for the glory of the Lord had filled the house of God."

The anointing has a residual component in it as we see in 1Samuel 19: 20 (KJV) "And Saul sent messengers to take David: and when they saw the company of the prophets prophesying, and Samuel standing as appointed over them, the Spirit of God was upon the messengers of Saul, and they also prophesied."

Saul sent 3 sets of envoys to capture David but in passing the company of prophets they all prophesied just as Saul did later on in the same chapter. How does this happen? It is what I refer to as a residential anointing. The strength of it can become so influential that the only choices are to conform as did Saul and the envoys sent or to detach. In either case it edges out the possibility of a familiar spirit setting up camp or strange fire goading its way in. The anointing can also be lost by way of having too much contact with people and places that carry a sin residual. It works both ways.

I recall 7 years ago a member of our church perished in a car accident. He was a native of Kenya. Much of his family had migrated to the states and settled in Texas, as his residence was in Kansas. When he passed it was decided that he would have a Life Celebration in Kansas City as he did, then in one Texas, and afterward his remains would lie in state in Kenya. Though I saw it in movies, it reinforced to me in real time how long distant travel for the deceased is navigated on the bottom of airplanes as cargo. In all respects I thought that it was eye-opening because the passengers who are living in most cases never know who's on the plane apart from the living.

The Anointing is similar to this, let me explain.

Should the engine of the plane fail, and lives are lost, the deceased cargo has nothing to lose. One could even argue that both the combined weight of the living and the deceased would have contributed to the failure of the engine. I want to say that when you carry the anointing you must be selective of the people you allow in your space. It becomes dangerous should they have nothing to lose. If they have an anointing that could be lost, then they'll operate on a greater level of caution and spiritual acuity in all life affairs. Whereas if they don't, behaviors can often be reckless, energy cantankerous while presenting a cynical aura.

Samson lost his anointing from a person who had nothing to lose, but 1100 pieces of silver to gain. He laid in Delilah's lap according to the Bible and according to Midrash and the Talmud he also laid in her bedroom too. *{WHEN YOU LAY AND YOU PLAY; YOU PAY.... "Preach Portley"}*

Our first interaction of the anointing points us to Genesis 8:11 (ESV), "*And the dove came back to him in the evening, and behold, in her mouth was a freshly plucked olive leaf. So Noah knew that the waters had subsided from the earth.*" This reveals that the anointing wasn't yet crushed in oil form.

The anointing is abused when we expect people to chew us as (olives) as opposed to pouring us as (oil). We must authenticate the process of the anointing as opposed to being synthetic imitations.

In love, I want to say that the church has become overpopulated with what I call the **BE** spirit:

- We have wannabes,
- Used to be's,
- Trying to be's,
- Has beens
- And maybes.

Lord, help your people!!

Being anointed does not immunize you from the dilemmas of spiritual pain. 2 Samuel 3:39, Berean Study Bible find David the king of Israel vulnerable as he states, "*And I am weak this day, though anointed as king, and these men, the sons of Zeruiah, are too fierce for me. May the LORD repay the evildoer according to his evil!*"

Many portray the appearance of maturity but operate in the adolescence of its anti-thesis. This is what I call "Spiritual

Voyeurism". We know that voyeurism is often associated with the practice of gaining sexual pleasure from watching others when they are naked or engaged in sexual activity, (Merriam Webster Dictionary). Spiritual voyeurism is a thing too. People often desire others to view them at a spiritual level in hopes of a stimulated representation and or an inflated reputation in return. I encourage all in this season to allow the Potter's wheel all the time it needs to perfect you. This way you're organic in and to the process. Speaking of the anointing let's examine the two passages:

1 Samuel 10:1, *"Then Samuel took a vial of oil, and poured it upon his head, and kissed him, and said, is it not because the LORD hath anointed thee to be captain over his inheritance?"* 1 Samuel 16:13

"Then Samuel took the horn of oil and anointed him in the midst of his brethren: and the Spirit of the Lord came upon David from that day forward. So, Samuel rose up, and went to Ramah."

These 2 passages revolve around the anointing of Israel's two first kings. Saul was anointed with a vial of oil whereas David was anointed with a horn of oil. The vial of oil was manufactured and put in a bottle meaning it took human hands to handle, tamper with and manufacture it. This is what I will call the Saul anointing. It is Man-made.

The horn of oil in which David was anointed came from a ram's horn. This meant something had to die to allow blood to be shed. This anointing was birthed in sacrifice because of the Blood.

Let me tell you this prophetically. You are anointed. Your anointing is about to take a major leap in dimension but as God prepares you for this transition stay clear of vial anointings, vial ministries and vial organizations. Easy, fast, and comfortable isn't always authentic or what's best. Wait on God's horn of oil to release to you what he has for you. This way no one can have what's yours. Samuel interviewed the anointing of the horn with all David's other brothers as his father's Jessie's suggestion. It wasn't for them, and it did not flow. The last, preferred by man, was first, chosen by God. The anointing has knock offs. Impressive energy, positive vibrations, charismatic personality, and virtuosic skill levels at a certain profession can be aspects of the anointing. They alone are not full proof of the anointing.

The anointing is also abused when there's an overindulgence with the gift of first impression. First impression is a gift some have and a gift many don't have. First impressions center around the genetic value of one's physical appearance. Some have this and to those that do you must be careful not to rely on this to do what the anointing was called to do. That would be abuse. Let me be honest before I go to the Bible. I have interviewed for jobs and if jobs and knew that I had a shoe in simply because I was a minority African American male. However, I balanced it. I did not allow that reality to settle for being unprepared, arrogant, big headed and overconfident in my approach prior to the interview. I knew that I tend to be more memorable during in person interviews than others, yet I'd still conducted a spell check on my resume and respected the time of the organization choosing to interview me. I'm saying that I know there are times that we all have natural things that work for us which is great but just don't stop at that.

A funny but true story is that my mother-in-law, Pam Brown, admitted to me that former president Barack Obama had her vote the first time she saw him. She conveyed to me that it was because he was tall, had a nice smile and attractive teeth. She said as long as he didn't do anything to drastically refute humanity's best interest that he was a president. In this case I believed that him being an African American helped him secure her vote as she by age attrition she's a baby boomer and has seen much in relation to racism, classism, and platitudes of long-awaited opportunity for minorities. All to say that "First Impression" works.

Speaking of King Saul, it worked for him too. Let's refer to 1 Samuel 9:2 (NIV): *"Kish had a son named Saul, as handsome as a young man could be found anywhere in Israel, and he was a head taller than anyone else."* He was identified as handsome, young and he was the tallest of all men at least by a head. This helped him. The fact that he had these attributes was not the problem as such attributes should not be viewed as problematic. The issue became sandwiched in reality, this was all he had. When put in a situation revolving around matters of the heart, the lack of heart he had was exposed. Let me speak to the contrary.

Eli the priest was morbidly obese and out of shape physically according to 1 Samuel 4:18 (EHV- Evangelical Heritage Version) [18]*"When the man mentioned God's ark, Eli fell backwards off his seat, which was by the city gate. He broke his neck, and he died, because he was an old man, and he was overweight. He had judged Israel for forty years."*

Not having the gift of first impression did not suspend his chances of becoming God's priest. While it's a bit appalling that it had to be a lack of self-restraint that took him out, it is also exhilarating knowing that it didn't keep him from being allowed to serve with a contestant's chance of advancement.

People are often drum majors for health advocacy when it comes to leadership selections. I'm for this as long as it does not ignore, negate, or frown upon God's choice. I'm not taking pride in the fact Eli was overweight I'm just saying that like myself some of us carry more love than we'd like to carry. (Listen Church, I'm walking heavy). Statistics say that most of us carry more caloric accumulation than needed. My takeaway is simply that even without the gift of first impression God can still favor you. So don't cancel yourself out or diminish your quality because of the lack thereof.

Zacchaeus was short in stature, but he made it into the Bible according to Luke 19:1-10. Yes, he had to climb the tree to see Jesus but, as a chief tax collector he was rich enough to purchase the tree that he climbed and own the forest in which the tree grew.

What about those 2 sisters in Genesis, yes, the daughters of Laban; Leah and Rachel. One had the gift of first impression and the other one didn't. However, the one that didn't have it was productive internally. Let's explore the passages. Genesis 29:11 (KJV), *"Leah was tender eyed; but Rachel was beautiful and well favoured."* Genesis 29:31 (NLT), *"When the LORD saw that Leah was unloved, he enabled her to have children, but Rachel could not conceive"*

Some time ago I preached on these bible passages using two visuals. The first visual consisted of a ham sandwich wrapped in a large Cheesecake Factory sack. The other visual was an expensive Rolex watch covered up by paper towels and then wrapped in a gas station plastic sack. The point was that most by propaganda would prefer the Rolex watch in value but would surpass it because of how it was labeled. While the other whopping majority would end up with a ham sandwich for dinner because their choice was motivated with ocular affections. We have to go beyond the surface as people of God if we are to escape the facade of a mere veneer impression.

Before our time together in this chapter dissolves might I mention the Apostle Paul, who did not have this gift impression either as 1 Corinthians 10:10 (NIV) states, *"For some say, His letters are weighty and forceful, but in person he is unimpressive and his speaking amounts to nothing."*

Ouch, I say ouch! Imagine someone saying this about you. I mean I'm not saying we are fighting, but we aren't cool either and I'm throwing some salt back in their eyes too. I will ask God for forgiveness later. Can I get an Amen? (*Relax… Just playing.*) This would not have sounded good to the ears of the Apostle, but it was a backhanded compliment that I'm sure promoted confidence that while he may not look the best in person, he was a Beethoven with his pen. I think God is saying we all have something though not everything. Work your something and let God anoint that.

So, before we raise up, I just want to say that A-Flat for me in relation to this chapter is simply the 'A' of anointing and authentication. Also, the 'A' for acceptance. Accepting who you may have desired to be but you're not. Canned greens properly seasoned can be good but will always pale in comparison to freshly picked mustard or collard greens cooked to perfection. Do they take more time? Yes, but it's worth the wait. Also, A-Flat to me stands for Acceptance. Accepting the purpose God has designated for you and not the role that others had in mind for you. Then finally accepting that though you may not be liked because you're anointing you also cannot be stopped either.

As the curtains drape over us concluding chapter 7, I want to leave you with some lyrics to a song that was among the soundtracks of my upbringing entitled "Anointing Fall on Me":

Anointing fall on me
Anointing fall on me
Let the power
Of the Holy Ghost
Fall on me
Anointing fall on me
Touch my hands my mouth
And my heart
Fill my life Lord
Every part
Let the power
Of the Holy Ghost
Fall on me
(Author: Ron Kenoly)

CHAPTER 8

The Aptitude of the Ancestors

In this chapter I'm going to discuss family chronicles on how bloodline contributes to who we are alongside our wills, ethics, and decisions. I want to disclaim that I love all people including family and friends. Family however is not always a biological connection. Many of Jesus' followers were not his family biologically as he stated in Matthew 12:50, (NIV): *"For whoever does the will of my Father in heaven is my brother and sister and mother."*

He saw family as those connected to purpose. In Matthew 13:56-57 (NIV) it states: *"Aren't all his sisters with us? Where did this man get all these things?" And they took offense at him. But Jesus said to them, "A prophet is not without honor except in his own town and in his own home."* "

The narrative further told us that he had to get out of the county of his home because it limited him. This enabled us to see how the biological connections presented struggles for even Christ. We're not exempt.

They also found offense in him. He did nothing, yet offense was found. Another way I'd say it, a voice of encouragement is that people who need to be victim at any cost are audacious. They often force conspiracies supposedly held against them that are not there. This gives the admission for the spirit of paranoia to reign and run rampage. The emphasis that THEY were offended. In cases like these there is usually a culprit who over time gains a heightened allegiance by evangelizing their contagious unconstrained emotions in others. I refer to this a satanic alliance with can come with doing a great work.

Aptitude circulates the idea of one's natural ability, but it also assimilates a spinoff with how generational bloodline can play a role in its determination. Sometimes the role it plays is a designation of mutual unity, other times it can be a cameo appearance genetically as other times a main character feature.

Additional words that promote the aptitude idea are words like innate, tendency, proclivity, inclination, hereditary and also inheritance. There are some families that are just predestined for greatness due to the brilliance of minds housed in their biological ecosystem. Then there are some that are expected to achieve at high altitudes due to qualified performances from previous ancestors in that family. That is a split decision. On one hand it can create pressure for the current descendants being compared to ancestry. On the other hand, the attention in regard to high hopes and support system is present at the on-slot should the descendants take the challenge of repetitive expectations. The unfortunate part is that this could also stifle personal aspirations that they may have beyond the shadow of what's expected from them.

Personally, I was always loud in laughter but quiet in thought. My thoughts poke vocally through my actions while my intentions were unsaid. One of the sneakiest things I did was that I learned about the natural proclivities of all the 12 zodiac signs, as well as the four classes of the 12 being cardinal, mutable and fixed. I say sneaky because I was taught against it in the church,

God was not said to function from such findings. My urgent inquiry to learn about the zodiacs spawned from 2 things.

To learn about why I was so austere, charismatic, spiritual, and daring, magnetic, sensitive, loyal, expressive, protective and oblivious, mysterious, lover of black, enemy of immaturity and fakes, and when angry, very cold. My point exactly! That's a lot to that going on, lol. It made much sense to discover that as a Scorpio I was an enigmatic and fixed sign. Not better or worse than the other eleven, just different and more complex.

The other reason being that as a minister I had married so many people. I counseled them accurately, prayed with and for them as well as was a good model yet they'd often divorce or separate. It happens, but it was at a higher percentage than it felt it should be.

I knew that there was more to it, as it was. It was a mismatch of signs. Love doesn't always mean compatibility, just as attendance at church didn't mean holy ghost filled. *(Stay with me!!)*

I had known about Regeneration according to Titus 3:5 (KJV) where it says, *"Not by works of righteousness which we have done, but according to his mercy he saved us, by the washing of regeneration, and renewing of the Holy Ghost"*

However, the believer must be washed and regenerated as in Regened, for old ways to not sabotage the marriage union. This is hardly church attendance.

Getting back to Aptitude; I felt like in my family on both sides that the unsaid target was to be great in ministry. I'm pleased to say per my view that the family has evolved as people, in perspectives and in expectations allowing everyone to be great in their own way. I also relished in the fact that God never needed the endorsement of family ancestors for approval of the descendants that he would raise up and in what ways he'd raise them. Like Jesus, some have to relocate their residence for their identity to find placement. Some need the college years and experience to confiscate back the privacy that close familial proximity prevented and alienated.

I know that I've mentioned my mom's death often as it was a turning point for me. At her demise all demanding bets were kind of off. I do live according to God's word but not so much by people's protocol and expectations. You have to arrive at such a place if you are to live out the script of grace that the Holy Spirit has carved out for you.

My genetic pool served me well. Paternally I took pride in inheriting a strong philosophical mind and being ethically sound in personhood. I also claim the paternal side as the source of my dignified charismatic charm. I was able to matter, being Michael the person above all else. Maternally I took pride in understanding the bureaucratic systems of power in the church. Also walking in the mantles of Levitical priesthood and music ministry. Honestly, I don't prefer one family over another. I see all the diversities presented as imperative necessities to grasp and opportunities to capitalize upon.

My advice to you all is pray about the hidden treasures of your bloodline and not to merely focus or magnify the generational curses. All families need prayer in some way as well; they are an answer to a prayer in another way.

All families in my view have to find the balancing act between what I call the "Jello (vs) the Jalapeños."

Let me explain. The Jell-O needs the additives of the water, the container, fruit and settling time. With the right alterations and fixations, the Jell-O is a phenomenal dessert. It represents the high altitude and aptitude with the aid of proper investments. It's much like an athletic superstar who has winning potential but never wins because the right pieces aren't surrounding him. When the front office of the organization understands this and spends the money to get the pieces around the superstar, they win. This is Jell-O. There's a piece of jello in us all. **Your condition is often greater by your company!!**

The jalapeño is quite different. It is independently pre-wired to perform at a moment's notice. There's nothing that has to be done to the jalapeno, just put it in your mouth and it's prewired to be spicy. The hotness is housed in its purpose. It was factored in its inception. Family genetics have a relationship similarly. Just like the spice cannot be evicted from the jalapeno, there are some attributes that God has pre-wired in you as a toolbox for purpose building and maintenance. **Stay away from people that consecutively demonstrate a hunger and a haste to cool down your spice especially when it's God-given!!**

In my family I struggled with feeling supported. I want to admit that I was a bit preconceived in my judgment. As a very young pastor I was in error as I measured how I calculated their love for me based on if they walked through the doors of my church independent of a reason. For two to three years straight secretly I watched that door to see if family would come worship with me. Don't get me wrong, it was a blessing to see newly acquired members come as well as older members who had lost their way and returned home. It was a blessing to see high school friends and college buddies come worship with me but keeping it a buck, I was bothered by not seeing family. Let me be honest. I wanted to demonstrate to them what had been taught and highly emphasized, which was ministry chemistry.

The more mature me is the mindset in which I encourage you with. I grew to understand that family technically didn't owe me support though I desired it. I also understood that there were a good number of family members on both sides that had prior responsibilities at their local church as well. True that but not so fast; I also retained the idea that some were not going to come just because it was me and maybe at some point doubted or struggled with my call.

Let me help you. Some people's regrets in life resurface when they see you operate in your calling. So, they avoid you. **What's often unsaid is often undeniable!!**

Absenteeism can also come from a place of them being compared to you by others behind your back. This means you can be unaware of the green-eyed monster of jealousy, envy and or competition. Family can sow carnal seeds among and against family. Also, there can be seniors in the family who by supporting you could leave them having to justify and explain why this one and not that one. It can get messy and political real fast. Too much of this energy isn't good for the ministry, family dynamics and or health.

Ultimately God was using this as seminary class to stretch and grow me. How so? Teaching me not to be so people driven, crowd pleasing and or socially dictated. Also, how to pivot in his direction independent of buy-in from anyone other than God and my immediate family.

There's an interesting passage in the Gospel of Luke I'd like to share. This is not to cast a stone or to indirectly throw shade. We find these words in Luke 14:18-20 (NIV), *"But they all alike began to make excuses. The first said, 'I have just bought a field, and I must go and see it. Please excuse me.'* [19]*"Another said, 'I have just bought five yoke of oxen, and I'm on my way to try them out. Please excuse me.'* [20]*"Still another said, 'I just got married, so I can't come.'*

It does highlight excuses of people which will always be a thing, but in a larger scope the intended message was meant for the master. Yes, it was about the master's ability to manage his temperament when things go wrong and when people's decisions disappoint you. The master who represents spiritual leaders, professionals and visionaries learned really fast that there's always someone who will break their commitment to you with premeditated stunts, schemes and or weak reasons.

Let me speak this over you.... "NEVER ALLOW PEOPLE BREAKING THEIR COMMITMENT TO YOU TO BREAK YOUR SPIRIT".

It may break your trust in them, but don't let it break your spirit. The master further learns that his anger changed nothing, and that people would be people. Listen, we have to allow for human space and human moments. The master finally learned that if his trust remained channeled and locked into to the Lord that there's always somebody that God has assigned to eat from your table. There's someone designated to be a part of your life as a witness and supporter. The key was this, sometimes your support is not from those that you've helped, loved, or supported. In many cases such as with this text the support was in the highway and the hedges as stated in Luke 14:23 (KJV): *"And the lord said unto the servant, Go out into the highways and hedges, and compel them to come in, that my house may be filled."*

My grandfather, the late Pastor and Superintendent, Reverend Moses Cofield Sr. would say, and I quote "Time is a fortune teller and, in the end, reveals all things." (*Preach grandpa*

Cofield.) He often closed his sermon in the key of A-Flat too, just thought I let you know that too.

I want to say that:

- Honor causes one to own their ancestral aptitude with grace and dignity.
- Wisdom allows one to accept the parts beneficial to their purpose, which parts to recycle, which parts rearrange and which parts to discard.
- Time causes one to understand who their real squad is as they are loved for who they are, not their contributions.

Before we turn on the porch lights allowing the sun to set on chapter 8, I want to share the 10 codes of time and how God allows them work for us while its day. Here they are enlisted:

1. Seconds
2. Minutes
3. Hours
4. Days
5. Weeks
6. Months
7. Years
8. Decades
9. Centuries
10. Millenniums

These Ten Codes of Times enumerated above were unanimously created by God for the purpose of seasons as stated in Genesis1:14 (KJV): *"And God said, Let there be lights in the firmament of the heaven to divide the day from the night; and let them be for signs, and for seasons, and for days, and years"*

All of the time codes revolve its evolution between Immediately and Eventually. Though it shares some tones of an obituary by way of the dash (-) of signified life span, we are reminded that time really is a gift engraved and engrafted to all species. However, the human species is most propagated and enhanced by the gift. Only what you do for Christ will last!

We have to become more laser focused on accomplishing what he's called us to do with intensity and intention. Many humans never get past number seven of the ten Time Codes (the average life span for many is between 70 - 79 years, if blessed).

This is a clarion call for all to no longer live the remaining time balance of your life in hurt, fear, or disappointment. We are simply not down here that long for such dysfunction. We are pilgrims passing through the earth hoping to leave it better than we found it. We must be economically fortified with the time we have and who we give it to. That being said I will say at all costs avoid "Time Thieves", both people and situations.

The Lord would go on to heal my soul from disappointment. I knew it because I stopped watching the church doors waiting on affirmation of family to walk in and affirm me as discussed earlier. This was also decorated with the continuity of love I displayed to those who never supported me. It took time as I do admonish you not to cheat the time it takes for true healing to occur. I was so healed that people who hurt me with years of absenteeism never knew they actually hurt me, neither did they ever receive a backlash from me.

Just because we function doesn't mean we're healed...

There are times when you're not healed yet you do have to function; in such cases own your triggers and limitations prior to involving yourself and you'll be fine.

A-Flat to me in this chapter connected the dots in relation to my shine. Prior to musicianship on the keys, I was seen as a drummer. So, to validate that I was no longer a drummer when I was asked to play at different venues on keys I would serenade with soft music, but I had to give my best presentation. I would give it the key of A-Flat. On another hand if you could play in this key as a musician in the family then you were ready to be used God. (Lol)

A-Flat, it was the subject that allowed me to matter as it secured my admission for familial adequacy and posterity notability. It also planted a solid substratum for which other parts of me were birthed.

Remember family, God has a way of advertising "this" in you for now, to secure advertising "that" in you in later years. It all works together. As we conclude this chapter let's be reminded of a portion of words to the hymn, entitled: "Hold To Gods His Hand"

Time is filled with swift transition,
None, none on earth unmoved can stand
Build your hopes on things eternal
And then hold, hold onto God's unchanging hand

Trust in Him, who will not leave you
What, whatsoever the years may bring
When your earthly friends forsake you

Still, still more closely to Him cling.

Everybody oughta hold (on to his hand)
Hold to God (God's unchanging hand)
Everybody outghta hold (on to his hand)
Hold on to God (God's unchanging hand)
His unchanging hand
Build your hope on things eternal
And just hold, hold on to to God's unchanging hand.

Source: Musixmatch
Songwriter: James Bignon

CHAPTER 9

The Alliance and the Antagonist

Every vision feed upon an alliance of committed personnel, organizational identity, and mission relevance for its operational purposes. Some of you all, like me, fly solo because it's your nature. Others, like myself, fly solo because of past snake bites (wolves disguised in sheep clothing betrayed you) or sheep bite, (the people you protected from the snakes that snaked you). Alliances have a common interest that often remains synergistically sound until some degree of success is achieved.

Success often gives embryonic function to **EGO**. Ego by acronym to me is: "Edging God Out" and or "Evicting God's Order". This occurs through the stimulation of thirst. Hungry people are motivated people that will work more intensely to achieve ethically. Thirsty people will undercut and backstab you in diplomacy with the hopes of replacing you; they kill you softly. Often in their effort to replace you they attempt to amputate and or discredit your relevance. Jeremiah went through this from the men of Anathoth, the village in which bore him as listed in Jeremiah 11:19 (NLT) when he says, *"But I was like a gentle lamb led to be killed. I did not know that they had made plans against me, saying, "Let us destroy the tree with its fruit. Let us cut him off from the land of the living, that his name be remembered no more".*

Strong alliances today usually consist of tribal heads who will pride their own alliances tomorrow. I speak from experience. They actually became apart to achieve, grow and then become. Leaders often can miss this because with the desire to become accruals their departure. Some don't miss it as much as they ignore it because they forget that while you can repeat seasons of victory it's usually not with the same faces.

Your confidants today are one opportunity away from becoming your competition tomorrow.

Separation doesn't have to be ugly, but rather it's the way it unfolds. Separation does have signals and suggestions of its coming prior to its occurrence. I refer to them as antagonists.

The Dictionary of Oxford Languages defines an Antagonist as a person who actively opposes or is hostile to someone or something, an adversary.

I would add to the permission and guidance of the Holy Spirit a semantic breakdown of the word. Antagonist-ant*tag*; so, I see it as a tag along with who doesn't have much better to do with time than to undermine and insult who they want to replace. Their small mindedness mirrors the limited stature of the ant, while their consistency to keep coming for you even when you didn't call for them mirrors the strength of the ant.

Antagonists meet us in every phase of life. What becomes the challenge is when they are assigned to your season. When this occurs, it is usually God using the antagonist as a processing station to birth characteristics in you that confidants and constituents would never get out of you.

Also, if we feel like being totally honest, God knows that our antagonists motivate us to some degree. It did with Jesus in Mark 2:10-11 (KJV) as a response to the Pharisees Jesus said, *"But that ye may know that the Son of man hath power on earth to forgive sins, (he saith to the sick of the palsy,)"*

"I say unto thee, Arise, and take up thy bed, and go thy way into thine house."

The man got 2 miracles for one (both spiritual & physical healing) and it had nothing to do with him but all to do with Jesus' motivation from that mouth of the antagonists. I often say it this way when preaching... "If they had shut up, maybe I might have given up." (Can I get an amen?!!)

Let antagonists be who they are without you changing who you are.

Henry Ford the maker, progenitor and CEO of the Ford vehicular industry has a story that tends to get lost in the shuffles of American History that I'd like to share. The Ford organization was an anomaly as its success was so glazed in grandeur that for multiple years, they really had no bonafide competitors. They were noted for high quality customer service. It was said that the magic to their customer service was that during the end of the interviewing process they offered a spaghetti meal. Whomever seasoned the food prior to tasting it wasn't considered for the job while those who tasted the delicacies first then made seasoning adjustments according to their liking were considered.

It seems Ford was after employees who were unassuming and optimistic opposed to assuming pessimists. I want to say that an Antagonist is one who seasons the food of your life with negative commentary without giving your legitimacy a fair taste prior. I refer to these types of individuals as complex personalities. It's almost as if they have to remain a defeatist to have a voice.

In Mark 5:9 (KJV) it says: *" And he asked him, what is thy name? And he answered, saying, my name is Legion: for we are many"*.

Legion spirits just don't appear. They are silent yet embryonic in the initial phase then grow in strength, confidence, and numerical influence over time. A Legion army consisted of 6000 thousand soldiers. I'd say that this was a strong alliance as they had one name "Legion." This worked until they were released to enter the swine, enabling each demon a new opportunity to have their own house as 2000 new housing units were now available. Even they don't get to be the head of the pig/new house they will support that house as an assistant. Either way, opportunity changed their viewing perspective. They were antagonists to the possessed man but an alliance to each other until opportunity separated their alliance causing them to antagonize each other for influence.

Jesus had Antagonist in his ministry and life just as we all will at some point. Again, we look at the most noted ones, which were the infamous Pharisees. They always had something to say and were seemingly committed to highlighting what they felt he did wrong.

I've come to learn that most antagonists have some degree of belief and or respect for you but struggle with the lack of control they have over you. Let me prove it! The Pharisees actually believed in the message of the gospel. This is according to Acts 23:8 (NIV), "*The Sadducees say that there is no resurrection, and that there are neither angels nor spirits, but the Pharisees believe all these things.*"

The Pharisees believed in the message but wanted the influence of him as the messenger. They believed in the foundational crux and feat of the cross, which was the Resurrection, but also angelic influence as well as the person of the Holy Spirit. I want to say many of your attacks are battles for influence. Likewise, I hold to the belief that external opposition is good for alliances of any kind. This includes family, religious, secular, and so on. I say this because of the war waging instincts that humans often wreak, as well as the unadmitted desire for attention. I conclude that this will be present regardless but better if channeled towards a common enemy opposed to each other.

It's like the World War (vs) Civil War. World obviously was a country in battle against another, while the Civil War was the same war but within and against its own kind. Paul the Apostle lends credentials to this in Romans 7:24 (NKJV): *"O wretched man that I am! Who will deliver me from this body of death? I thank God—through Jesus Christ our Lord!"*

He noticed that when he went to do good that evil was consistently present. Evil's potential never took off days, snow days or vacations. It had perfect attendance, while the good, intended nature was often on sabbatical, medical leave, on sick days and or FMLA.

What the Apostle was addressing was the dynamic between the ENEMY apart from the INNER ME. We blame the ENEMY for things that the INNER ME was responsible for.

We must not make the common mistake of breaking rank to win an argument or to be right proving a point. This alters the vision of any kind and can create unsanitary motives because opposition becomes more of the focal point than accomplishing any type of greater good.

Joel 2:7 (American Standard Version) speaks to the importance of maintaining rank:

"They run like mighty men; they climb the wall like men of war; and they march everyone on his ways, and they break not their ranks"

Ranks are important and nothing can entice you to break it like the innate need to prove a point as in the raged desire to be understood. Ranks are easy to lose and in the Spirit are only achieved authentically. So always think about the price paid to get where you are.

Before we look at rank biblically let me share a story about a fight for life between an aged cat and possum. The cat wanted a meal, and the possum wanted a fight to survive the cat's hunger. They start fighting as the possum goes down in defeat though it fought hard. The cat begins to eat the possum but because of the cat's age coupled with the fight the possum gave it the cat became winded. While the winded cat attempts consumption of the now deceased possum, the cat suffocates and chokes to its death. Within ten minutes they had both died. The question is who won the fight?

My response is that there was not a winner but only a first-place loser (the cat) and the second-place loser, the possum. The cat only is the first-place loser because the possum never had the knowledge of knowing that the cat died too.

This is how breaking rank works. When you come down to the level of your opposition you become like an ostrich bent over, you expose your neck; *here a Chop, there a Chop, everywhere a Chop Chop.* As for the antagonist they retain the rank they had while being messy, while if not wise, you lose the rank you had proving a point. It's never worth it.

Let's look at rankings biblically. Let's recall what Samuel said to Saul upon Saul's preparation for anointing. Though Saul was God's choices he still had to come up to the level of God's man

Samuel the seer. As God was using Samuel to invite Saul up to a higher rank as King, Saul's mindset had to undergo a shift as he was instructed go up to the High Place. This was not just geographical, but rather a geographical place in representation of a higher rank in the Spirit.

1 Samuel 9:19 (KJV), *"I am the seer," Samuel replied. "Go up ahead of me to the high place, for today you are to eat with me, and in the morning, I will send you on your way and will tell you all that is in your heart."*

Samuel tells him to go alone first. Meaning that there will be times in elevated situations when you have to go alone and stand alone as he did.

Then there was Moses who by the aid of his father-in-law Jethro was advised to stop breaking rank as it would contribute to physical breakdown and mental fatigue.

Exodus 17-18, 21-22, (KJV):

[17] *"And Moses' father-in-law said unto him, The thing that thou doest is not good."*

[18] *"Thou wilt surely wear away, both thou, and this people that is with thee: for this thing is too heavy for thee; thou art not able to perform it thyself alone."*

[21] *"Moreover thou shalt provide out of all the people able men, such as fear God, men of truth, hating covetousness; and place such over them, to be rulers of thousands, and rulers of hundreds, rulers of fifties, and rulers of tens:"*

[22] *"And let them judge the people at all seasons: and it shall be, that every great matter they shall bring unto thee, but every small*

matter they shall judge: so shall it be easier for thyself, and they shall bear the burden with thee."

Sometimes we break rank because we can be control freaks. Let's talk about this. Are we okay with designations and delegations of people that we lead that may be stronger than us in some areas?

Can we let others shine and use their gifts without the silent fears of having to share kudos? Does heartbreak from years ago disable trust in others today whom God sent to help build our vision? Do we have the humility to take advice from modern day Jethro's who may not have our qualifications, proficiency or portfolio yet they utter the wisdom needed?

This is food for thought, that we must sort through and deal with, in pursuit of our best version. This part perhaps is not the fault of the antagonist but the leader of the alliance.

Let me borrow one more witness before the chapter benediction. That witness is Jesus while being transfigured. He knew that he didn't have ground level Glory so in order to maintain his rank he had to invite the selected three up to him. He knew that on their level he was a decent human, but on his level, he was a Divine Hosanna as we see in Matthew 17:1-2 (NIV): *"After six days Jesus took with him Peter, James and John the brother of James, and led them up a high mountain by themselves. There he was transfigured before them. His face shone like the sun, and his clothes became as white as the light."*

He invited them up to his rank, but the access pass was not unlimited, it was by appointment, and it was abbreviated. They could only inhale so much at his level, so he kept them at visitation status.

Side note: **DON'T GIVE RESIDENTIAL ACCESS TO PEOPLE WHO ARE VISITATIONAL IN CHARACTER!!**

Many of our problems come when we offer too much access without restrictions. You must not allow the antagonist to see your nakedness or become too common. I have to go here because it is often a missed detail in the recorded documentation of King Hezekiah. I love King Hezekiah's testimony as it did advertise God's response to prayer and his ability to grant healing by way of extended life as was the plight of this king. However, in the appendix of his life after the healing, he demonstrated much ignorance that became fatal all because of a break in rank and a braggadocious need to show and tell the bounty of his amassed prosperity. His ambitions for this were so amplified that he disclosed classified information to the Babylonian envoys who were generational enemies to Yahweh.

We see this in Isaiah 39:2-7 (NIV): *Hezekiah received the envoys gladly and showed them what was in his storehouses—the silver, the gold, the spices, the fine olive oil—his entire armory and everything found among his treasures. There was nothing in his palace or in all his kingdom that Hezekiah did not show them."*

Then Isaiah the prophet went to King Hezekiah and asked, "What did those men say, and where did they come from?" "From a distant land," Hezekiah replied. "They came to me from Babylon." The prophet asked, "What did they see in your palace?"

"They saw everything in my palace," Hezekiah said. "There is nothing among my treasures that I did not show them." Then

Isaiah said to Hezekiah, "Hear the word of the Lord Almighty: The time will surely come when everything in your palace, and all that your predecessors have stored up until this day, will be carried off to Babylon."

A-Flat in this chapter ebbs and flows on the idea of the antagonists. When I would often play music anywhere as well as church the crowd was made up of different types of people, namely 3 kinds....

1. **FANS/** that are commentaries. They are loyal to those winning and attracted to behaviors that certify a winning status. Don't slip and fall off because fans will leave you for who's up without notice and often no remorse.

2. **FOLLOWERS/** These are emotionally connected to you. They represent the more integral set of a company. They do not make you stronger in many cases but in most cases, they don't limit you either.

3.**FRENEMIES/** enemies who are friendly. You've had lunch with these people. They want success and your become their motivation due to similar skill sets and roles played out in your lives. You usually only get this kind of person to talk to if and when you fall short, but very seldom to congratulate or compliment.

The eagle teaches us that he has enemies at times called sparrows. He learned that if he maintains his rank by soaring high that the sparrow can't survive air at the altitude level that he can. Hypothetically, eagles are members of a unified alliance while the sparrows become the antagonist. I want to say the antagonist can't do anything to you if you just keep soaring. As we fade out of this chapter preparing for the next, I want to leave a portion of lyrics to a song entitled, "Wind Beneath My Wings".

Did I ever tell you you're my hero?
You're everything, everything I wish I could be
I could fly higher than an eagle
For you are the wind beneath my wings

Oh, and I, I could fly higher than an eagle
For you are the wind beneath my wings
'Cause you are the wind beneath my wings
Fly, fly, fly away, you let me fly so high
Oh, you, you, you, the wind beneath my wings
Oh, you, you, you, the wind beneath my wings.

Source: LyricFind
Songwriters: Jeff Silbar / Larry Henley

CHAPTER 10

From Almost to Already Done

I want to initiate this chapter with the bravery of much candor and without any fear of retribution. Simply put, anything that "almost" happened, 100% did not occur. If I almost got the job; then the organization, I interviewed with is totally not my employer. If my truck almost started today, it didn't start. If I almost got released for jail, I indeed still have a prison ministry.

Y'all get me yet? Okay just a couple more.

If the children are almost potty trained, keep buying baby wipes and Huggies.

If your NFL team almost made it to the Super Bowl, then you can always call it a rebuilding year as they will watch the Super Bowl. (Lol).... last one...

If he's almost handsome and she's almost cute, then they both need.... Well, you know?

Ok, Let's work!!

"Almost" is a season that I'd dare say that most have experienced. Frustrating as it can be due to not closing in on tangible and testimonial manifestation, it does permit one to discover the neighborhood of possibility. Almost is a proximity that's literally spitting distance from within a winning season. Almost is almost having a good hand when playing cards, maybe not a great hand but not a poor one. One could even lament that it's compatible with a left hand. Left hand suggests a puncher's chance to knock out a fighter who is much more skilled than its athletic minority while in a contested bout.

In the days of mythology as well as in Bible days your disability made you infamously famous as it preluded your identity. This was so with the mythical god Hephaestus who had a disability that hindered his motility crippling his mobility.

"He was depicted with curved feet, an impairment he had either from birth or as a result of his fall from Olympus. In vase paintings, Hephaestus is sometimes shown bent over his anvil, hard at work on a metal creation, and sometimes his feet are curved back-to-front: Hephaistos amphigyēeis. Hephaestus - Wikipedia"

One irrefutably could win the argument as to why he should serve in a coveted role with such a limited capacity to execute physical responsibilities. Well, to God disabilities are not disqualifiers

This was closely related to Artaxerxes who was said to have a disability. In depth studies have verified the validity that one of his arms was half the length of the other. This is said to have fortified the necessity of Nehemiah who was employed as the King's cupbearer.

Nehemiah 2:1b (NIV): *"In the month of Nisan in the twentieth year of King Artaxerxes, when wine was brought for him, I took the wine and gave it to the king."*

Why was he allowed to serve as king?

Well, again to God, Disabilities are Not Disqualifiers.

Then there is Jonathan's son Mephibosheth who is introduced by way of his disability every time his name is mentioned. The first time he mentioned his name is not quite known but his limitation was as seen 2Samuel 9:3 (KJV): *And the king said, is there not yet any of the house of Saul, that I may shew the kindness of God unto him? And Ziba said unto the king, Jonathan hath yet a son, which is lame on his feet.*

In the archives of American mindset and philosophy we learned that being born with a left hand was viewed as a disability. People born left-handed like me were often forced out of the habit. While the majority of right-handed individuals were encouraged to enhance their use of being right-handed. Some scientists hail the belief that left-handed people are capable of a more "diverse range of thinking", stemming from creative imagination. American History tells us that 8 of the 46 presidents were left-handed.

These 8 lefties are not listed to reprimand the remaining 39 right hands. It just offers fair play to the equality establishment.

Here they are:

James Garfield

Herbert Hoover

Harry Truman

Gerald Ford

Ronald Reagan

George H.W. Bush

Bill Clinton

Barack Obama,

This means that half of them were labeled as disabled by society, yet they emerged to the highest office in the world as the President of The United States. I would also say that this made them increasingly versatile because being forced to learn with your right hand as a leftie does not disable the use of natural ability with your right. It makes you ambidextrous.

As the POTUS' all of them have a very requirement that demands brief ambidextrous use as they are simultaneously sworn in with their right hand in the air and their left hand on the Bible.

Those left-handed presidents would go on to sign treaties, law binding documents, legislation agreements and Congress approved Bills of Rights… all with a left hand.

I've had my share of "almost" moments. Some made me cry as I often thought of a master lock padlock that would only open with proper combination. The combination would have 3 reversing turns landing on numbers. You could have the first two right and the last one so close, but not land on an accurate number and the lock would not open. A miss was a mile. These occurrences too often can be a few things at work. Let me expound.

1. When we find ourselves consecutively landing in almost territory it can be that we are not paying attention to detail. Details often make a difference. Paying attention to detail forces us to operate more in facts over feelings. Though feelings do matter they can also be detrimental to our potential. Some deals and opportunities you can't leave open. They must be communicated in agreement, in time considerations, along with proper response, social etiquette and high efficiency with how they're handled. Implementing this advice makes you closer opposed to a procrastinator. For example, God can be swinging things your way spiritually, but that doesn't remove the fact that a full voicemail box can nullify such opportunities. Someone may capitalize on that opportunity simply because they check their voicemails frequently and respond accordingly, whereas the more befitting person didn't pursue the details.

2. The other thing at work here is that God can be guiding your voyage and monitoring your destiny by way of misfits and mismatches. I believe that God knows that all humans have an innate desire to believe and belong, and well as give love and receive it. So, he allows mismatches in relationships, and opportunities because he knows that we'd stay there. He knows that we'd build a house where we were supposed to pitch a tent. Just as God did not allow Abram to get too comfortable with his family or to be successful where he was, because if he does then Abram never leaves at the time God commissioned him to. If

he never leaves, he never acquires the God's wealth package, he never would've received the promise of descendants or become Abraham. He would've died Abram, which is a picture of average. God has more for you than average. So, accept the consecutive mismatches and misfitting as signs of future assignments in greater territories.

3. Finally, and statically people like safety so much to a point that whatever is out of their comfort zone can't be of God and vice versa. Baskin Robbins Ice Cream was known for having an extensive catalog of 31 flavors. Over the years that catalog of flavors has ballooned to a library of over 1000 flavors. These flavors are distributed between 6000 plus locations worldwide. What's interesting to me is that the vanilla flavor has always led the pack in sales demand. Why is this? I would say because people like safety. Those such as I, we go in and sample the new flavors and, in most cases, love it but we still go with what was the familiar selection. In this season your faith will have to be put in practice in greater measures because where there is no risk there's no reward. I love to teach this way: **Faith is like film; It is developed in the dark.**

Baskin Robbins have some flavors only available on the East coast, other flavors can only be found in the Midwest. Certain other flavors are only found in the West, but vanilla flavor is everywhere. Some things you have to be in intentional pursuit of or you will never inherit them. A lack of faith makes for a boring person and life. Together let's reignite our faith at once.

Some situations were not reflective of an insufficient effort on your part but perhaps the other parties involved. We saw this in

In Acts 26:28 (KJV), *"Agrippa said unto Paul, "Almost thou persuadest me to be a Christian"*

Paul had no error in the situation as it was a matter of Agrippa's heart. So, there are times to be patient with yourself knowing that your assignment was only to plant seeds while another will water it and God in time gives the increase.

Recapping the left-hand discussion is closely connected with the idea of a remnant, because it deals with what was left. This pandemic has left many ministries, industries, organizations, and households operating with a LEFT HAND, almost reliving the depression of the 1920s. We must remember that despite Hells demonic agenda that God has us in the hollow of His hand.

Paul the Apostle references a conversation between God and Elijah, in Roman 11:3-5 (KJV), *"Lord, they have killed thy prophets, and digged down thine altars; and I am left alone, and they seek my life. But what saith the answer of God unto him? I have reserved to myself seven thousand men, who have not bowed the knee to the image of Baal. Even so then at this present time also there is a remnant according to the election of grace."* (It's all factored in God's will).

God was in the process of updating his own reputation in relation to his name credibility. He does this by leveling manifestations to what was deemed impossible.

This was similar to Jeremiah 14:7 (NIV), when it was stated, *"Although our sins testify against us, do something, LORD, for the sake of your name. For we have often rebelled; we have sinned against you"*.

So, I want to speak into your life and let you know the phases that God is using to bless you.

SOON.

Many of you all have passed this phase in your process as you've been waiting and praying for change. It's like the Ice Cream Truck that you hear but can't see. It's near and will soon drive by.

SHORTLY.

This suggests that the blessings prayed for are closer yet indefinite. The Ice cream truck you heard you now can see it but it's servicing another client in your neighborhood. Their testimony indicates your next will shortly become your now.

SUDDENLY.

The place when you recognize that if you have the faith God has the power. Such faith can move mountains and immediately call in the miraculous simply with the heart of faith and authority with the mouth's decree. At this point the Ice Cream truck of favor has arrived at your home. (Thank you Jesus).

Let me say it another way; God will also confirm his favor in you using this process.

AFTERWHILE.

Simply put you know it is coming and all delays will work in your favor.

ANYDAY.

It's been shipped to you in the Spirit, you're just awaiting natural time to catch up with eternity. Don't count it strange to wake to a life altering email or to receive a text message of a lifetime opportunity.

ALREADY DONE.

This is the conversation of a faith junkie and the intended manifestation of a persuaded intercessor. Worry, fear, doubt, depression, or anxiety have no chance here. (Thank You Jesus).

The word "almost" in Greek is the word "schedón" where we get the English word "schedule". This can suggest that some of the missed opportunities you had would have thrown you off schedule. Not all things good are all things God! Jesus never sinned yet the Spirit drove him to the wilderness. The wilderness in some cases as with Christ confirms you are on schedule going through it, while detouring it can put you off schedule. So, the feeling can't indicate scheduling.

{Really quick, here's a true story}:

A few months ago, Kansas City transitioned out of Winter into early Spring. One day it rained in the morning, and I'd worn a light jacket. By noon the sun had come out so that the jacket was unnecessary. Around 3:00pm pieces of hail came out of the sky for about 25 minutes. By 5:00pm there was a tornado watch coupled with even colder air than that morning. This was all on the same day. The point here is that the weather changes the feeling of climate; and that how one feels is never a true barometer of what season you're really in.

Schedules are appointments orchestrated by God and our behaviors do one of four things.

1. Causes what is on schedule for us to lag in delay. (Consecutive distractions)

2. Causes what's on schedule to be canceled. (Consecutive willful sin, whether it's private or public, or whether you're admittingly glad of it or shamed by it)

3. Causes what is on schedule for us to arrive at the intended date. (Focus, patience, and submission)

4. Causes what's coming to be advanced. (Maturity and authoritative faith)

In the Spirit I want to declare that your life is on schedule with God's agenda. I want to encourage you to do what's not so easy at times and that's to *speak* and *believe* in the Sovereignty of God despite contrary evidence leveled against your current life experiences. For those that it seems like you're in a season of economic downturn and that the spiral that was to create opportunities has dug a ditch, get ready for greater. By faith that ditch may be for someone but not for you and yours... "In the mighty Name of Jesus!"

Before we conclude let's discuss the reversal clause of "Almost" and how it presents Already.

Almost has a reversible clause that works in the benefit of our good. For example:

If I almost died; my life was unequivocally spared.

If I was almost unemployed; that means I still have a job.

If I almost relapsed and or overdosed; I still maintained my sobriety.

If I almost gave up; that means I stayed grounded and grinded it out.

If I almost lost my mind; that mind is still in a position for God to blow it.

This happened in Luke 10:30-31 (NIV), as Jesus told a parable, "In reply Jesus said: *"A man was going down from Jerusalem to Jericho, when he was attacked by robbers. They stripped him of his clothes, beat him and went away, leaving him half dead"*.

It said the man was left " half dead" after a life-threatening encounter of violation from a robber. The portrait that Luke illustrates is one of bleeding humanity that was six inches north of a homicide. This was really bad to a point that I don't want to risk vindication of such a vindictive assault. That being said, the blessing was that HALF DEAD is represented as fully alive.

This is how we must approach our 'Almost' in order to get our 'Already done' on full display.

Life in the Key of A-Flat here caused me to rethink how advantages came from disadvantages. I became a fluent musician that was left-handed. It was very awkward at times. The advantage was that I learned how to walk the keybase with the edge because I was left-handed. I learned to manipulate the keyboard from the vantage point of left to right. Musically, being left-handed blessed me, but it had seemed to curse me first. So, as it is in life as the pressure in life squeezes us, but it often squeezes flavors, skills set, potentials that we didn't know existed.

As we conclude our time in this chapter, I want to leave a portion of the lyrics to a song arrangement popular by Mary Mary entitled: "Can't Give Up Now"

… I just can't give up now

I've come too far from where

I started from

Nobody told me

The road would be easy

And I don't believe He's brought me this far

To leave me

… Never said there wouldn't be trials

Never said I wouldn't fall

Never said that everything would go

The way I want it to go

But when my back is against the wall

And I feel all hope is gone

I'll just lift my head up to the sky

And say help me to be strong, oh

… I just can't give up now

I've come too far from where

I started from

Nobody told me

The road would be easy

And I don't believe He's brought me this far

To leave me

Source: LyricFind

Songwriter: James Cleveland, Warryn Campbell, Trecina Atkins, Erika Atkins

CHAPTER 11

Alligator Advancement

In this chapter I'd like to discuss how we can advance as victors in life even when opportunities we had were not capitalized upon or well stewarded. My shared observations are hinged on a story that left me baffled and totally intrigued. As a student of National Geographics and a nature enthusiast, I've always studied human behaviors and its relation to natural instincts graded by one's intuition. As graphic as it may seem this story deals with reptilian ingestion and gets close to the practice of cannibalism.

This first visual is one that displays a crocodile being ingested by a snake. Snakes as we know squeeze their prey to the point of suffocation. Then when this is achieved, they then swallow the victim whole as their boneless body structures and stretchable teeth pangs allow them to do. Notice here though how geographical vicinity played a role. It was on dry grassy ground. This played into the favor of the snake as he quietly slithered his way into his meal. The alligator could've prevented being swallowed had he made the snake come to or near the water where he's more versatile and resourced. We must not be so quick to engage in war, anxiously leaving the principles and territory of the church. Had Mr. Alligator done this then either the snake would lose its life in battle or spares its life by reneging on the confrontation. Oftentimes those we should have converted convert and then consume us.

Let's try this as a memory tool: SIN FASCINATES, THEN IT DOMINATES, THEN IT ASSASSINATES.

We cannot use carnal weaponry or mentality to fight spiritual wars as we are reminded in 2 Corinthians 10:4, *"For the weapons of our warfare are not carnal, but mighty through God to the pulling down of strong holds"*

Grief and Gloom are often dictated by geography. Many shootings, rapes and several other menacing activities that leave innocent casualties to be mourned and or restored often occur near and in places that brood negative energy. At the risk of stereotyping ones preferred lodging locales of entertainment I won't name examples. However, I will say this this, "TO STAY

OUT OF THE SEAS OF SIN YOU MUST STAY OFF THE BANKS OF TEMPTATION."

The banks of temptation are usually where the fish are caught. This most likely occurs by way of a response of opening our mouths at times when it was best not to. The fish is pulled up out of the seas onto the bank when caught. He's caught simply because-- "He Opened His Mouth." Humans have a similar playout, but it's reversed. The human is pulled into the sea from the banks because of an opening in their mouth. I often say that the mouth has a feature called tongue that is located in a slippery place and from time to time its subject to SLIP.

SLIP as in very (S)arcastic, at times to (L)ax, (I)gnorantly exposed and to (P)rovocative with word.

The banks should be avoided at all times. Samson ignored this as many of us may have. According to his Nazarite vow he was never supposed to touch or kill the lion, but it wanted the honey and ignored the honor he owed his vow.

Numbers 6:5-6 (NIV), *"All the days of the vow of his separation there shall no razor come upon his head: until the days be fulfilled, in the which he separateth himself unto the Lord, he shall be holy, and shall let the locks of the hair of his head grow." "All the days that he separateth himself unto the Lord he shall come at no dead body."*

He also had timid accountability as some do. This occurs when sin is ignored if what can be gained by the sin works in their interest.

Judge 14:9 (NIV), *"He scooped out the honey with his hands and ate as he went along. When he rejoined his parents, he gave them some, and they too ate it. But he did not tell them that he had taken the honey from the lion's carcass".*

I don't blame his parents solely for his actions though they could have administered inquiry but didn't because their sweet tooth had needs. (Listen)!

This second visual displays the clever instincts, intelligence, and courage of the alligator. Let me explain what happened.

The alligator was swallowed by the snake and has been overcome but is not quite dead. He's as close to death as you can be without complete succumage. It is here where his instincts, intellect, and instincts tag team with his will to live. As one of only a few species that can slow their heart rate down to 2- 3 (bpm) beats per minute without actually dying, this alligator does this. As he plays possum, he's got the snake fooled making it think he's dead. This is survival at its best because the snake has left killer mode and transitioned into digestive recovery mode. The alligator knows he's got a final chance at life so he's cautious on when and how to force exit. At once, with teeth and claws harmonizing their aggression with haste he protrudes out of the stomach of the snake disfiguring the snake's intestinal organs until the alligator is secured and the snake is finally and fatally decommissioned.

This has several takeaways. The few I'll share are these.

1. What do you do when you fail to subdue modern-day serpents with your feet as we are authorized to in scripture according to Luke 10:19 (KJV):

   "Behold, I give unto you power to tread on serpents and scorpions, and over all the power of the enemy: and nothing shall by any means hurt you."

   Yes, it was the Lord's intention for us to tread and trample upon them with our feet. Meaning that we never were intended to be on the same level with them, let alone end up in their stomachs. However, in real life it can happen to us as it has many. When this happens what do you do?

   Let's watch this alligator because in my revelation of this explanation he became a modern day Jonah!! The prophet Jonah was swallowed by a fish that God prepared as a consequence for his disobedience. The God whose instructions he ignored was the same God he prayed to in crisis. Some situations have a way of realigning the humility in us that we've squandered in a way unprecedented. The alligator as well as the prophet Jonah are products of those who wouldn't listen to as they should've, ignoring warnings that prelude destruction, yet God mercy was still enduring enough to reach them. Come on now family, we've all been there, and the Lord reached his hand grace and snatched us out of the fire as stated in Jude 1:23 (ASV), "*And some save, snatching them out of the fire; and on some have mercy with fear; hating even the garment spotted by the flesh*".

Though it was by way of the BPM, the alligator changed his heart. We must have a change of heart when the grip of death's jaws intends to sharpen. The alligator's change of mind, twinned with a change of heart, knocked the wind out the snake attacking its internal stomach, where its core is located. The clincher here is that the enemy has no CORE muscles or values, so attacking him with the core values of the Kingdom victory will always open up exits of deliverance.

2. The other thing he did was wait until the geographical scenery changed. The first visual was when the alligator was overtaken and consumed. The second visual was when the alligator reclaims his life but waits until the snake was much closer to the water where his residential abode of safety was. The water was a sign of life but especially for alligators. The alligator to me was comparative to the prodigal son in Luke 15. After he had been shamed and swallowed by sin. The Bible says that he came to himself leaving the world and he went back home. Luke 15:20-

23 (NKJV), *"And he arose and came to his father. But when he was still a great way off, his father saw him and had compassion, and ran and fell on his neck and kissed him. "And the son said to him, 'Father, I have sinned against heaven and in your sight, and am no longer worthy to be called your son.' "But the father said to his servants, 'Bring out the best robe and put it on him and put a ring on his hand and sandals on his feet. And bring the fatted calf here and kill it and let us eat and be merry."*

That said, there are just some environments that you can't engage in and retain your focus free from the secondhand smoke of distraction. It's not that such environments are sin as much as they resemble the banks of temptation.

3. The final observation drawn from the alligator was that every person has a weakness. In the case of the snake, it was a defect. The snake, as volatile and vile it is the reality is that it doesn't have legs or arms while the alligator does. This makes the universal saying true "He's been unARMed and permanently deFEETed". (Selah).

    The alligator also has no feet. Let's think about this, in the passage of Luke 10:19 we were commanded to tread upon the scorpions and serpents. Metaphorically speaking it's only our feet that would allow this. So, we are instructed to use our feet to step on an enemy's head who has no feet. It's a fixed fight. I used to often watch WWE (wrestling program) on television as it was a therapeutic deposit for me. It wasn't until I attended a match in person that the word of the Lord comforted me as I do you. I always knew that the matches were predetermined but I saw while being there that the action was real. It was like 5 men sitting adjacent to the ring as the matches switched off and, on the gains, and losses of momentum. The crowd had become emotionally involved, but these men were never moved. Why? It was because the fight was fixed!! So it is with us. What you've gone through both now and in past times are real events, but the fight is fixed in your favor. I know you feel the drop kicks, body slams and that you've sustained the choke holds, but know it's a fixed fight if you stay with the Lord.

In the final visual the snake has swallowed a sheep. This is listed to remind us to keep our foot on the enemy's head and to stay away from his mouth. When this sheep strayed away for us Shepard it was gobbled. The old story reminds us that the

Sheppard would anoint the most sheep with oil. The oil served as a repellent against snakes that would hide away in the holes as opportunists. The oil scent would fade off without the renewal of anointing. Some of us may have strayed away from our chief Sheppard the Lord Jesus, but we have to find our way back home unharmed from a plethora of satanic devices. This is only achieved by way of being obedient, attentive and submission to the good Shepherd, our Lord Jesus Christ.

John 10:14-16 (NIV), "*I am the good shepherd; I know my sheep and my sheep know me just as the father knows me and I know the Father and I lay down my life for the sheep. I have other sheep that are not of this sheep pen. I must bring them also. They too will listen to my voice, and there shall be one flock and one shepherd.* (AMEN),

A-Flat in this chapter resurfaces ministry performances that didn't go so well in the beginning. All victories in life are not promising at first glance. In these performances the movements were weak, the instrumental arrangements at times were fatigue, my focus was distorted, and the vibe was off baseline. I could either scratch it and start over or live with an average outcome which is tough for me to do. I knew that at some point in the performance that I'd get an opportunity whether given or created to solo. Solos then were referenced as my time to "testify". A solo was your time to improve with improvisation. I was testifying with my solo, but I was also making bitter water sweet. I was communicating an apology musically for having a bad start. I would do this until the room changed and the joyful energy surged back into the ministry performance. While it wasn't about me, I did have the control switch at that time to make sure what started off rocky concluded in joyful bliss. As the alligator was in the center of the snake's stomach, I want to conclude this chapter with a portion of lyrics to a song entitled: "Center of My Joy"

(Verse 1)
When I've lost my direction, you're the compass for my way
You're the fire and light when nights are long and cold
In sadness, you are the laughter, that shatters all my fears
When I'm all alone, your hand is there to hold, ohh

(Verse 2)
You are why I find pleasure in the simple things in life
You're the music in the meadows and the streams
The voices of the children, my family, and my home
You're the source and finish of my highest dreams, woah

Chorus
Jesus, you're the center of my joy
All that's good and perfect comes from you (all that's good and perfect)
You're the heart of my contentment, hope for all I do
Jesus (Jesus), you are (you are) the center (the center) of my joy

Source: LyricFind

Songwriters: Gloria Gaither / Richard Smallwood / William Gaither

CHAPTER 12

Being Astute is Knowing When to be Aloof

In this chapter I will share explorative insight on how to tactfully handle shrewd and political personalities that you may encompass towards your pursuit of victorious living. This is done with the execution of being astute.

According to the Oxford Language Dictionary, "astute" is having or showing an ability to accurately assess various situations and people while implementing ways to turn this to one's advantage. Many confuse being astute with being eloquent. They do have some similarities but are different because an eloquent person knows how to speak. That doesn't mean they know how and when to be quiet. Saint Paul taught that verbal rest was a discipline of delicacy that every child of God at some point should demonstrate use of.

I Thessalonians 4:11 (KJV), *"And that ye study to be quiet, and to do your own business, and to work with your own hands, as we commanded you."*

Some confuse astuteness with knowledge. They too have connecting points, but they differ due to knowledge being what you know. Every professional quarterback can throw a touchdown pass in practice but can't always produce this when under the pressures of game time. Knowledge is a winning ingredient as it is power, but singularly it doesn't always win.

I always explained it this way.

1.   Knowledge: Is simply information

2. Understanding: Is Comprehension

3. Wisdom: is the Application of both

Therefore, astuteness is a conglomerate of all three drizzled with cleverness and the sobriety of alertness. It's like when most kids grow up and they make their own fountain drink mixing all the flavors. We called it a suicide. So, it is with Astuteness as it is a fatal drink to ignorance and a euthanasia that provides numbness to dumbness always giving itself the distinct advantage.

Astute people have always intrigued me as they taught me how to be patient. They can be so patient at times that you'd almost think they forgot their endgame when indeed they hadn't. They had just mastered a few things, namely their mouth, their emotions and ambitions. What they mastered they use moderately; they just don't allow them to lead. They know that the very things that make you special can also create avoidable suicide if and when there's overindulgence.

Remember this: Manage to Master Your Appetite, or Your Appetite Will Manage to Master You

We have to find the space that blends astuteness with ethics. While I settle on applauding astuteness because it is a milestone of brilliance, an exhibition of restraint and balanced ambitions, it also can be a millstone. A millstone that causes the milestone to fade in glory, deducing its flagship to a mere pole.

I don't want to stay here too long but I'm crawling in this hole for just a moment because many people too often pursue astuteness independent of spiritual guidance and moral compass.

When this happens, all it takes is for one to want something bad enough and they will go to an un-resigned measure to fulfill it.

Being astute can have a nocturnal component attached to it. Nocturnal meaning active and motivated by the night. I also think it can mean people who manipulate situations through others without their motives being disclosed. This is not so much the physical darkness of the night, but the darkness of the heart shadowed in the battlefield of the mind. Dangerous is a person who commits a crime, but more dangerous is the one who negotiates the crime mentally through the mind of others. We saw this through King David.

2 Samuel 11:14-17 (NIV), *"In the morning David wrote a letter to Joab and sent it with Uriah. In it he wrote, "Put Uriah out in front where the fighting is fiercest. Then withdraw from him so he will be struck down and die."*

"So, while Joab had the city under siege, he put Uriah at a place where he knew the strongest defenders were. When the men of the city came out and fought against Joab, some of the men in David's army fell; moreover, Uriah the Hittite died."

Wow! If a man after God's own heart can be taken down by such malicious ambitions, we must know that if we don't stay on guard that the enemy will work us too.

This was really gangster of David! He made sure there was no blood shed on his hands; he made sure Bathsheba was an available widow that he eventually married and even though the first child died they later had another child, Solomon. David was judged for his actions. I get it, but who cried justice for Uriah's innocent corpse as he was carried and buried to the tomb of earthly finality?!?! Again, I say that was gangster.

There was another gangster biblical episode that was nocturnal in mindset. We find it in Genesis 33:1-2 (NIV), *"Jacob looked up and there was Esau, coming with his four hundred men; so he divided the children among Leah, Rachel and the two female servants. He put the female servants and their children in front, Leah and her children next, and Rachel and Joseph in the rear."*

What was going on in the text was that the two twin brothers Esau and Jacobs quarrel had mounted into a 20-year feud. The feud had festered into a cadence of silence between them. Now they are meeting for the first time, and they really don't know each other's state of mind. Esau is accompanied by 400 men. In his coming, Jacob in a fit of urgency divides up his children amongst his babies' mamas'. Yes, I said what I said.

They were positioned in the order of compassion that he had on them. Who he loved most he put in the rear increasing their chances of survival, should there be any bloodshed, and so on. The love and lack thereof he had for the babies' mamas dictated the love levels he displayed for the children. This was pathetic! This was all done on top of impregnating two biological sisters (yikes). This was very astute of him yet gangster and nocturnal in mindset.

To balance astuteness, we must see it as a secular trait of a blank canvas. Secular meaning that its use of it sways it to the left of sinfulness, or the right of sacredness. Like social media it's a good servant mechanism that either has good or bad front office management. Some restaurants I loved the food but my future interest in returning defaulted due to poor social health with the customer service. Other places the food was just okay, but the customer service and culture were amazing, so I returned. So, it is with the use of secular characteristics.

Let me shift as I share what I consider to be the protein of this chapter: There will be seasons when God places you in environments where you're not the leader, yet you have influence and, in some cases, the greater weight of influence. Tough slot! Tough Spot! If not astute the pot can get really hot!

Positions of power are not always given to those best suited. I believe with all my heart that leaders awarded positions of power from gaming, politicking or nepotism know that purely motivated influential people are threats. The threatened demeanor of that leader leaks overtime as the influence is revealed organically in those being led. We often acknowledge the student who desires to replace the teacher but do not always circle around to the intimidated lion of leaders who are intimidated at the growth of their cubs. They would be fine if only the cubs would remain cubs and never evolve, or if the cubs grew at their approval and endorsement. That's not how it works and because of this many leaders attempt to suspend the influence of their threats by discrediting contributions made with asinine commentary. Have you ever seen someone work really hard to ignore you and all the wealth of grace and gift that comes with you? The same leader prefers and often elevates those who can be controlled, but they tag the label with "I think they're the best fit for the organization at this time."

These are the moments you must keep the faith and use such scenarios as signs that your breaking out season is nearby. What do I mean?

Exodus 2:3 (KJV), *"And when she could no longer hide him, she took for him an ark of bulrushes, and daubed it with slime and with pitch, and put the child therein; and she laid it in the flags by the river's brink."*

Moses was hidden by his parents. When they lost control of his growth spurt, they sent him down the river. When people attempt to hide your value and magnify your flaws it's only proof that your bursting out season is near.

This is many of your issue as you've been called by God and the enemy seems to desire to afflict your spirit, don't worry because IT'S ONLY A SIGN OF YOUR MIRACLE EXPLOSION!

When you have the influence but you're not the leader, here's my instruction for you: Honor the leader, as it is a mirror reflection of how you honor God. This also ensures that your favor won't be stunted. Saul was intimidated by David as he thought David wanted his job. David had the influence and Saul was aluminized with aggressive bouts of hate for no reason. The influence of David that bothered Saul most was when the opposite gender threw up in his face. This reveals possibly whose attention he was seeking.

1 Samuel 18:7-9, [7]*"And the women answered one another as they played, and said, Saul hath slain his thousands, and David his ten thousand."*

"And Saul was very wroth, and the saying displeased him; and he said, They have ascribed unto David ten thousands, and to me they have ascribed but thousands: and what can he have more but the kingdom?" [9]*"And Saul eyed David from that day and forward."*

The women said it, not David. This was an illusion of Saul as well as a displaced deposit of anger management. Saul attacked who could replace him, not who pointed it out (Ahhhh). This is how the enemy operates, though angered by who set the alarm off (the women) he went after the threat (David).

I once preached a sermon entitled " Beyond the Sets" which graded one's capacity apart from universal desires. Here was the breakdown.

S. - Style

E. - Entertainment

T. - Taste

S. - Socialization

The message I intended to push was not to allow the "sets" to be all your made up of and the only thing you live for. Partakers of the set do not cross a sinister boundary neither should it be frowned upon with its engaging in. In fact, without them life is dull, dreary and decomposed. My encouraging and objective argument was to not allow the SETS to totally dominate you. When there's nothing else to talk about these discussions have been had then I'd challenge that person to dig deeper within their soul as there is a more of a glossal extension to their purpose that is yet to be identified. This is also known through the contrasting of the SETS, for example

S. - Style/ is awesome but it must include substance to be substantiated over time.

E. - Entertainment/ is necessary at times but over time without education, it's like dust after hitting the water.

T. - Taste/ as in consumption is great, as I'm actually *good* at it(hello), but consuming with planting, sowing and making investments in various with always conclude in impoverished survival

S. - Socialization has biologically, spiritually, and scientifically proven to be a therapeutic necessity. Also, with being social, having moments of solitude is just as important.

Now, I enumerated this because being Astute often includes knowing when to be Aloof. Don't let your right hand know what your left hand is doing. Blend in with the sheep.

The Dictionary of Oxford Languages defines Aloof as: *conspicuously uninvolved and uninterested, typically through distaste.*

When there's an inconsistency with ethics being exemplified from those in power, this will not be exciting to those waiting on the Lord to advance you. So you have to know how to go along to get along. Your assignment may not be to correct, it may be to pray; or wait on God to remove tension; or to be an advocate for another God may be preparing to advance.

Being aloof decreases the attention that has a tendency to work against you. There's a saying you may have heard or even repeated which is "When in Rome Do as the Romans do". If not taken out of context I think the saying has teeth. In doing this you have to vibe verbally on the treads on commonality. The main reason for mentioning the SETS, was because they become the conversational material used to draw small talk from. This doesn't make you fake, it's the mindset of the favored, neither does it make you weird but rather wise. Many of your adversaries take more of a diplomatic rather than disrespectful approach but your demise is still their endgame. I took the longer route home explaining this because in the Spirit influence is being reassigned in the Body of Christ. Seats of power are changing for sure, but in some cases while seats that are becoming available parlay themselves into vacancies influence is usually transferred first.

So being astute is being aloof but it also requires the intellectual wherewithal to know that while God is raising you it's often around and in front those that may have beef with him because of his selection of you. These new opportunities can occur gradually, as at other times moderately to immediately.

Finally, the SETS are vitally important to catalog and pull from when needed, especially if there's a tendency to say too much. KNOW YOUR TRIGGERS!!

We all know people with great potential but are apprehensive of becoming too close because they have too much say. In love, I refer to them as having a "BREAKING NEWS SPIRIT". This refers to individuals who take much pleasure in being the carrier of news. It can be accurate news but maybe shouldn't come from them. It can also be false news but as long as they have an audience that will massage their adrenaline they will spill. They cut you off mid-sentence for fear you will share something that they want you to know they knew first. They have all day to talk but often have very limited time when listening. You have to be careful of this kind because they just want to be first to report commentary often at any expense. The astute person can't model this as it often will expedite one's removal from favor as it exposes motive and confidentiality breaching. People with a "Breaking News Spirit" often lose density over time.

It is much like the word "Supernatural." It has a spark to it. However, if everything becomes 'Supernatural" then its commonality enforces a deductibility in the demand that it had. This makes what was Supernatural now natural because what was astonishing and astounding became anemic over time. What was once a powerful soar is relegated to a pedestrianized comparison. So, it is with "Breaking News". When there's Breaking News to Break this News, then more Breaking News to break that news, and some more News to Break this News after a while it just becomes "News". What was once epic shrank interest. So it is with these types of people. They seem to have a lot of rope but often they hang themselves.

As we break down the equipment set up for chapter 12's symposium I want to say that being astute includes effective discernment of time. We saw this with the sons of Isaachar in 1Chronicles 12:32 (ESV), *"Of Issachar, men who had understanding of the times, to know what Israel ought to do, 200 chiefs, and all their kinsmen under their command."*

Though the smallest tribe in tribal heads were tough leather, small pieces are a bit strong in punch.

Impeccable timing leads to unrestricted success. On average it takes four arrow sticks for the anesthesia to work on a male adult lion. They will work in 10 to 20 minutes putting the lion down. There is a space there where the Lion is tapping out to the anesthesia but if you assume he's totally out just because he's down. He could still kill a human. I want to say that sometimes we make the right decisions but at the wrong time. We have to pray for discernment at the same level we pray for our desires.

A-Flat in this chapter takes me back years ago to a time when I was invited to play and vocally lead a mass congregation in the singing of the "Lift Every Voice and Sing" anthem. I did well with my rendition on that day, but the people were not as involved like they were 3 years later when I was asked to perform the same task. What was the difference? It was my evolution. I had learned to implement astuteness which was to understand that the congregation was to become one sound. The prior 3 years I exhibited extra chords and bonus unnecessary notes both vocally and instrumentality. I knew that I had a shot at being on the evening news with the performance, so I took the risk of being seen and heard leaving the chorus line. I never made it to my 5-

minutes of fame on TV that year either. That's what I get for being thirsty!!

Within the next 3 years following the first performance, I learned to respect the music, especially the standards, hymns, and anthems. I had executed 'astuteness' approaching it with 'aloofness' meaning I performed with the responsibility to showcase Black History and not myself. I won that time because I was willing to blend in with the forest, not having to be the tree.

As we transition into chapter 13,

I want to conclude with the lyrics of a song made popular by Pastor Shirley Caesar entitled: "You're Next in Line"

You're next in line for a miracle
Your breakthrough
You're next in line for a miracle
You have kept the faith
Today is your day for a miracle
You're next in line for miracle
Your breakthrough
You're next in line for miracle
You have kept the faith
Today is your day for a miracle

Today is your day
Today is your day
Today is your day
Take by faith, take it by faith
Today is your day

Take it by faith, take it by faith
Today is your day for a miracle.
Written by: Michael E. Mathis and Shirley Caesar

CHAPTER 13

The Adjunct, The Adjutant and the Accomplished

In this chapter I want to reinforce how being faithful pays off. My hope is to encourage you the readers to demonstrate utmost vulnerability giving in to the Sovereignty of God. This accredits validity but also veracity to Hebrew writer to this scripture recorded in Hebrews 10:23 (KJV):

"Let us hold fast the profession of our faith without wavering; (for he is faithful that promised;)"

Upon my own interpretation an "Adjunct" is an additional component added to a pre-existing and functioning organizational system. Their services are more supplemental than they are primary. In reality the adjunct professional though helpful to the cause is usually the detail that's cut first when budgeting is down. Adjuncts are more or less part-time employees without benefits or promissory commitments from their employer. Their skill sets are just as sharp as anyone else but the organization usually for various reasons has not made an agreement to fully endorse them with a premier hiring package. This may be due to a plethora of reasons including a grid lock in cap space, apprehensions with stability and or them not being viewed as a viable necessity. I say this to encourage you because many times God's presents you as an 'adjunct average' to get you in the door, but that's not how the story ends.

I often think of acting guru and musical savant the multi-gifted Jamie Foxx and his humble beginnings. He's been a consistent blessing to the comedic and cinema world, though it seems to me that he was presented as an Adjunct actor. Opportunity by opportunity he began to stand out during the sitcom "In Living Color".

There were others on the set of the show whose careers were on schedule for a rocket fueled success and did well from that open door. Jamie Foxx however was unanimous in his response to the world's reception of him as he orbited that opportunity into albums, recurring sitcom series, comedy tours, movies, radio appearances as well as being the host and feature on some of the most opulent stages known to man. It's not a competition but looking back at where he started many would not have assumed that he would have emerged over all others as he did. Life's too short to carry bitterness as it can be a tendency to disdain the ones who were selected for the choicest rank over you. Sometimes this is God as it was in John 9 when the disciples of Jesus asked him a question that typical humanity would have. Grounded in assumption, laced in pessimism, and submerged in bodacious audacity they asked whose sin caused this man infirmity?

John 9:2-3 (NKJV), *"And His disciples asked Him, saying, "Rabbi, who sinned, this man or his parents, that he was born blind?" ³"Jesus answered, "Neither this man nor his parents sinned, but that the works of God should be revealed in him."*

Let's chew this down a bit. They were asking if it was "generational" as in his parents' sins or was it "situational" as in his personal sins.

It was neither! God just wanted to show up, show out and show off His Glory in the man's life.

Just be the adjunct and prepare for the desired season while God is crafting scenarios to work in your favor. Samuel the seer was an adjunct King that was never officially appointed. At that time Israel was a theocratic in structure (systematically governed by God's pleasure through Samuel's prophetic call). The nation became democratic (governed by the people's influence though the monarchy of a King).

Though never appointed as King there was something remarkable said about him in relation to the persistence of his spiritual vocation. It was the phrase "None of his words fell".

1 Samuel 3:19 (BSB), *"And Samuel grew, and the LORD was with him, and He let none of Samuel's words fall to the ground"*

This is huge taking into account how many false prophets we saw in the Bible days as well as present day. **"It's better to be an authentic adjunct than an artificial accomplishment"** *(Selah).*

Samuel functioned as God's mouthpiece anointing, appointing, and terminating kings. He was an auspice to the position of king but never sat in the seat. This reminds us all to play the part assigned to us in that season because, "ONE DAY WITH FAVOR OVERPAYS PAST SEASONS OF LABOR"! (Speak Lord!)

Adjuncts in the kingdom require higher degrees of faith because without the mantle of the appointment there's no stipend factored as it for the kings. David angered God with this mindset as the tendency was to look to the people (horizontally) for his bounty opposed to the Lord (vertically). We saw this in 1 Chronicles 21:1-3 (KJV), *"And Satan stood up against Israel, and provoked David to number Israel.*

And David said to Joab and to the rulers of the people, Go, number Israel from Beersheba even to Dan; and bring the number of them to me, that I may know it.

And Joab answered, The Lord make his people an hundred times so many more as they be: but, my lord the king, are they not all my lord's servants? Why then doth my lord requires this thing? why will he be a cause of trespass to Israel?"

God was upset as David was looking to the numbers to guarantee the wealth security of Israel, while God through faithfulness would always make numbers count.

Just as Jamie Foxx goes from being an average charming adjunct with mere cameo performances that metamorphosed into a star-studded mogul, so can it be with you. Little really becomes much when placed in God's hand. Jamie goes on to win an Academy award in 2005 for best actor in the film "Ray".

Then we have the "Adjutant" who has similarities with the adjunct but still separately identified. What is the role of

Adjutant? According to the Dictionary of Oxford Languages it is - *an officer who assists the commander of a military unit. In British and Commonwealth armed forces the adjutant is the principal administrative staff officer of the commander of a battalion, battle group, regiment, squadron, or military post.*

In the mindset comparisons of faith, an adjutant is a leader serving a leader. In most cases motivation is driven from an innate desire to become more. And yes, I know it's as unto the Lord. True that, but let's be honest, much of servantship is often driven by the hopeful future winds of opportunity and tossed in the waves of proper timing to attain more.

Adjutancy is a fancy word for Assistant. Though camouflaged in protocols it's a role that signatures itself in servant leadership. This is often given synonymous names as such: Administrative Assistant, Executive Assistant, Pastoral Assistant, Associate Director, Managers Assistant and so on. The point is that this can often put you in a position where your one heartbeat of a person away from the throne. Let's look at Theodore Roosevelt, who was the 26th president of our nation. According to Wikipedia:

"Roosevelt assumed the presidency at age 42 after McKinley was assassinated in September 1901. He remains the youngest person to become president of the United States."

History sketches the reality that Roosevelt was likened to an Adjutant Assistant to the president. He never knew that McKinley would be assassinated but he had prepared himself to discharge the office at an exquisite level. This initial adjunct role would expand him into a record-breaking age being the youngest to serve in that role (42). Though John F. Kennedy (43) was the youngest elected president, It was Theodore Roosevelt who was the youngest to assume the role and was an archetype for those appointed in their prime years. This was additionally impressive, understanding that he was only 7 years removed from being illegally too young, as you had to be at least 35 years old. 35 was an older age then as the life expectancy was much shorter then when compared to now.

The Adjunct became the authentic Accomplished by waiting for the right opportunity and properly stewarding prior preparation for it.

Really quick, let's leave information for inspiration. Many of you are "trees" that God has planted, and you are on course to accelerate any day now. By acronym, to me <u>TREE</u> stands for:

Trusted & Teachable

Reliable, Real & Reachable

Ever Evolving

Enduring

Let's look at two types of Trees,

Weeping Willow Tree

Weeping willows experience the fastest growth, (often grown in Asia) but they are very shallow in root structure. When the wind really picked up, the roots couldn't hold the trees in the wet soil, so down they went.

Then there's a Bamboo Tree:

After it is planted It doesn't break through the ground for five years (that's 260 weeks, over 1800 days) After five years, once it breaks through the ground, it will grow over 90 feet tall in five weeks!!

When Hurricane Irma Hit Florida, The Bamboo Trees Survived It!!

Beloved you are the Bamboo tree you are built beyond breakage. You are storm proven as you will outlast it. You may not have a closet full of suits or a paperback bible in every car, but may I say that to you that- A SLOW GROWTH THAT'S

Confirmed Is Better Than a Fast Growth That's Only Tentative!

We have a lot of tentative Christians, that are maybe saved, sometimes sanctified, casual in belief, and occasional in their standings. We also have tentative people who are afraid of risk, intimidated of the first glance of trouble and that becomes escapist to friction. I want to say that your reservations for greatness are no longer tentative but have been confirmed by God. This is what the Psalmist was alluding to in Psalms 1:3 (KJV), *"And he shall be like a tree planted by the rivers of water, that bringeth forth his fruit in his season."*

Solomon in Ecclesiastes also ministered to us when he declared in Ecclesiastes 9:11 as I paraphrase, "The race is not awarded to the swifted, the gifted or the lifted, it's not awarded to those who can quote 60 scriptures in 60 minutes; The crown goes to those who've ENDURED. Some of you were broke but you Endured; sick and tired but you Endured; divorced and betrayed yet you Endured; lied to, broke and depressed…but you Endured; alienated but you Endured, working two jobs just to barely make it, but You ENDURED.

There was another president whose metabolism was slower than the others as he weighed in at over 330 pounds which was extremely morbid obese in the mid-1800s. This was William Taft, our 27th president. Once rumored but eventually taking on a skeletal reality was that Taft had gotten stuck in his bathtub due to rapid weight gain. While this is said to be intriguingly true there are also lessons, we do well to pull from it. While on your journey as an adjunct in route to your season of accomplishment the enemy will often highlight your fallacies and failures. Using Taft's life as fountain to parachute hope from I'd say this:

1. It's better to break a bathtub attempting to wash dirt from yourself than it is to let dirt accumulate. Have you ever met someone who had a squeamish scent and was unpleasant in smell so long that they no longer could smell themselves? Shhhhh, I won't tell! I will say that getting stuck in the tub is much greater than getting stuck in the toils of sin. At least he was willing to wash. We must be the same way.

Proverbs 13:44 (NLT), *"Godliness makes a nation great, but sin is a disgrace to any people."*

2. If I were a betting man, I'd presume that he was stuck due to giving cleaning emphasis to certain parts. Though we have over 2000 parts as humans, not all carry the same odors of attrition. As far as the church I think we've become guilty of pouring bottles of water in the ocean.

3. The church giving life to the church is necessary at times. However, it is the sick who needs a physician and the dry places that need more of the moisture of God's word. This visual reminds us that the ocean being poured into will not benefit from the watery offering. It simply will bank it for later, while statically according to Cholera – WHO (World Health Organization) dated Mar 30, 2022, 3-4 million people die annually from dehydration.

    Maybe the idea is right, but the appeal is to the wrong audience. We see it more clearly when seemingly someone else who is already blessed keeps getting blessed while you're still waiting on the same prayer request to mature into a praise report. We don't say but we think it is. Taft's tub teaches that even in washing and become clean of sin that there will always be a narrative that invites details that contribute little to nothing.

Finally, according to Wikipedia:

President Zachary Taylor, a general and national hero in the United States Army from the time of the Mexican American War and the War of 1812, was elected the 12th U.S. President, serving from March 1849 until his death in July 1850.

As death would evade him at age 65, we learned that he died while on the toilet stool. Yes, you read that correctly, I'm not repeating it! (Giggles)

Real talk fam, President Taylor suffered from "cholera morbus", a stomach illness deemed as an indeterminable cause.

I highlighted his cause of death because much like the visual of the water, if we give accurate diagnoses but to the wrong patient, then the patient who needed the treatment fatally expires. We must not allow the world to die of internal mess that they were trying to evacuate from but didn't because they had no deliverer.

Romans 10:14 (KJV), *"How then shall they call on him in whom they have not believed? and how shall they believe in him of whom they have not heard? and how shall they hear without a preacher?"*

The Adjunct and Adjutant in closing are positions of humility that God often uses as a canopy that drapes over and amour bears the process of dominion birthed from discipline. Accomplishments will find you on its own terms. Many times, what seems late in our eyes is on time in God's eyes.

A-Flat for me in this chapter has much to do with learning why some performances went sour after much effort given in preparation. It was one thing to have a poor performance because of a lack of self-care for my voice and or not effectively studying the music instrumentality, but what was hard for me to swallow was that poor equipment contributed to poor performances. My skills grew to a point where I couldn't assume that the venue and in most cases the church had the proper equipment. While some did, most didn't. The lesson was that just as I had invested into my gift, I also had to invest in proper gear that would support my skills sets. I had graced many churches, funeral homes, wedding facilities and so many of these organizations did not upgrade or update their sound and or instruments. I didn't care about this for the longest until the prehistoric equipment crippled my ministry presentation. I was never for the fluke or mere appearance of acquiring the latest equipment without the commitment of practice. I always believed in, DON'T STEP OUT AND BUY (upgrades), UNTIL YOU FIRST STEP UP AND BE (practice commitment). I grew to learn that it is important to make sure you're not just heard but also understood. The toughest part here was the evolution in mindset that guided me from a novice to a professional. Investment is a part of what makes you a professional and not just the skill set. Likewise, it's mutual, it's not just the equipment upgrades either. The gear along with the gift supports overall growth. The gift and gear grow together as they work in concert aiding each other.

As we lock the doors on apartment chapter 13 and make ready to move in studio chapter 14, I want to leave you with a portion of lyrics to a song entitled: "It's Your Time"

You've been faithful, you've been true
And you've done all that you can do
And for your faithfulness, it's your time
You applauded for the rest
Now it's your time to be blessed
And for your faithfulness, it's your time

You've waited for so long
But you held on, and you were strong
And for your faithfulness, it's your time
You encouraged everyone else

When you needed it for yourself

And for your faithfulness, it's your time

You encouraged everyone else when you needed for yourself

and for your faithfulness; It's your time!

Source: LyricFind

Songwriters: Luther Lee Barnes

CHAPTER 14

Alienation, the signal of Awareness preparing you for future Acquisitions

In this chapter we will examine how alienation can be used by God as a sign of divine calling upon one's life. As the thesis unfolds here is a scriptural foundation that we can draw fresh water from.

1 Peter 2:9 (KJV), *"But ye are a chosen generation, a royal priesthood, a holy nation, a peculiar people; that ye should shew forth the praises of him who hath called you out of darkness into his marvelous light:"*

The definition of Holiness is to pursue active separation from worldliness.

Alienation by definition features a loss, a lack or a removal of sympathy experienced from an entity; it's an estrangement as well as a form of isolation. All human life at some point is forced to deal with alienation. Some of it can be self-imposed as other times influenced externally. I find that there can be a weird space when one does not fully comprehend why they must endure certain paths alone, yet they know they must. I refer in large part to these times as being "Navigational Transition". This often results in consecutive rerouting that God often sanctions. Reroutes never surprise God. Never! They can be due to sins consequence just as they can be a path carved out by God himself. Many often despise the reroutes until we think about the ones that hurt us, straight up looking you in the whites of your eyes and pulling off a convincing lie, and those that betrayed us. If honest we'd invite the opportunity to reroute being connected to them in many cases.

Reroutes can cause you to feel as if your journey has been abandoned by the abundance of goodwill as well as cause you to acquiesce to frailty of mediocrity. Universally speaking, l dare to assume that when most see the REROUTING SIGN, that mild adrenaline is magnified by the irrevocable loss of time, the worrisome fear of late arrival to one's destination and gasoline waste. This can be exhausting and draining but let's not forget about Cindy Godley, the September 11th survivor. One could argue that her case augments restorative belief in Rerouting and how at times it's a badge of honor that can serve as a saving grace.

According to The Chronicle a portion of the article stated:

Even 20 years later, the anniversary is still challenging, Godsey said this week.

"I do want to get back to where the towers were and what they've built. I have not done that yet. At some point I will go back there. At times, I think I'm going to do it. I don't know that I'm ready," she said. "There are some people that say, 'Well, you know, it's been like 10, 15 years.' And yeah, I understand that. But when you're that close to you actually almost being in it, it's just ... some years are easier than others."

She believes God had a hand in her narrow avoidance of death two decades ago. In 2000, her mother's mother-in-law and Godsey's father died within three weeks of one another.

"God wasn't just looking after me, he was looking after my mom," she said. "I just don't know that she could have handled."

Alienation, though proof of the call on your life can cause you to resort to an identity crisis. These times are pivotal as you cannot lose yourself by becoming overwhelmed in overthinking or overreacting. The earth and the world need you, so you can't lose you! There are 3 parameters that I would suggest grading your sobriety by.

IQ/ Intellectual Quotient:

The mental grasp one has in regard to their faculties ability to house understanding and to adequately distribute reasoning.

EQ/ Emotional Quotient:

How one manages their passions, sensitivities, and feelings, namely while in a quandary of fiery affliction.

AQ/ Adaptability Quotient:

How you respond when things that were unplanned playout in various ways without notice, permission, or desirability.

While all 3 are fiercely imperative to effectively manage I'd motion that Adaptability is most crucial as the EQ & IQ can be sharpened, suppressed, and confronted by yourself and or close circle. However, the AQ occurs spontaneously and extemporaneously. Most people can pass the exam on two of the three while one of the areas needs more attention.

Which of the three would be your area of opportunity to grow?

For myself personally I needed patience from those who loved me from the EQ level. I'd say " I'm cool" when something bothered me but what I really meant was that I'm going to be okay. In reality I was hurt, blood was leaking from my spirit and hope was hemorrhaging as if it were a vapor from my soul. I'd pray and it helped for a while, but the malady of spiritual arthritis would eventually return in splinter form. Prayer and therapy I learned were the best antidote when administered effectively, but at the time my maturity wasn't there. What helped was television.

Stay with me. Over the years my favorite sitcom was the "Martin Lawrence" show. I'd often ask myself what it was that made his show so iconic in my view. I first thought that it was his ongoing feud with Pam who was Gina's best friend, or maybe the even-tempered voice of reasoning of Tommy, or the loose screws of Cole's ignorance. (Lol). Those were factors but I realized what it was after years of watching it. I had finally discovered that I had a small crush on the 9 different characters that Martin played apart from him playing himself. For years this had impressed me and over the years it was educating me. Here are the 9 different characters he played.

1.Otis
2. King Beef
3. Jerome
4. Elroy Preston
5. Edna Payne.
6. Dragonfly Jones
7. Roscoe
8. Bob
9. Sheneneh Jenkins

Again, it was the characters and the lessons that I had gleaned from them. Martin and the cast did their job as they entertained us. However, the mistake that one could make is if they tried to live out in real time what was meant to entertain. What I mean is that we often when alienated attempt to play the role that will "unalienate" us. (Selah).

When that role loses its steam then, next! Next and again next. This repetitive cycle can be vicious to one's self esteem and wreak havoc on one's nervous system. All of the roles Martin played were hilarious to me with my favorite being Dragonfly Fly Jones. So, my takeaway in no way is an indictment of the show as it is my all-time favorite. It just reminds me as I do you, that we often undertake identities that will applaud us, but it can also ignore who we really are. I would say it this way, it is better to be hated for being your authentic self rather than to be celebrated for being a carbon copy of someone else.

As child I was always intrigued by my dogs as well as the neighborhood dogs as they would use much of their spare time chasing their tail. This was strange:

The lesson we learn here is that dogs spend their whole life chasing their tails. At the day of death, it can never be put on their obituary that it was caught (Selah).

Activity alone is the knock off imitation for progress! Progress leads to effectiveness; however, activity alone produces "Adrenaline Junkies". Safeguard your time, values, and identity. Move in peace on purpose, not in popularity, prediction, or propaganda.

We also can see that the dog is not only chasing its tail but also its "past" as the tail is located behind the head where the mind is located. The mind represents currency while the tail represents the past as justified by the release of bile and its defecation. Yuck, I already know, but the truth is…. Sometimes uncertainty is God's way of removing you from having access to the control switch. As long as you have control then God can't take pleasure as stated in Hebrews 11:6 (NIV), *"And without faith it is impossible to please God, because anyone who comes to him must believe that he exists and that he rewards those who earnestly seek him."*

This has happened to me before when I would be willing to trade in a much better future of uncertainty for a past hindering season of certainty as we saw with Israel's words of pessimism to Moses in Exodus 14: 11-12 (NIV), *"They said to Moses, "Was it because there were no graves in Egypt that you brought us to the desert to die? What have you done to us by bringing us out of Egypt? Didn't we say to you in Egypt, 'Leave us alone; let us serve the Egyptians'? It would have been better for us to serve the Egyptians than to die in the desert!"*

Little did they know they were actually in spitting distance of a miracle as Moses the mediator would respond back to their condescending chatter.

Exodus Chapter 14:13-14 (NIV), *"Moses answered the people, do not be afraid. Stand firm and you will see the deliverance the Lord will bring you today. The Egyptians you see today you will never see again. The Lord will fight for you; you need only to be still."*

Alienation was also how God would conduct circumstantial surveys that statically revealed his choice of you, as stated in John 15:16 (KJV):

"You did not choose Me, but I chose you and appointed you that you should go and bear fruit, and that your fruit should remain, that whatever you ask the Father in My name He may give you."

I'm convinced that even some of the prophets in the Bible would be diagnosed as Mental Health patients by today's standard. These are the very ones who were set apart as mouthpieces declaring the oracles of God. Come on, Jeremiah metaphorically became a human fountain dispenser as he cried multiple times a day.

Jeremiah 9:1(NIV), *"Oh, that my head were a spring of water and my eyes a fountain of tears!*

I would weep day and night for the slain of my people".

God also never granted Jeremiah the privilege to marry. This could be taunting as well as an eternal ouch moment as his desires for companionship were terminated. I'm not referring to just physical activity but also having a vessel of trust, a confidant, a committed witness to his vocation, and yes even a family to secure the seed of his posterity.

Jeremiah 16:1-2 (NKJV), *"The word of the Lord also came to me, saying, "You shall not take a wife, nor shall you have sons or daughters in this place."*

Then there's Jonah who spouted temper tantrums because God wouldn't destroy the nemesis nations of his ancestry. Jonah 4:1-3 Contemporary English Version (CEV), *"Jonah was really upset and angry. So, he prayed: Our Lord, I knew from the very beginning that you wouldn't destroy Nineveh. That's why I left my own country and headed for Spain. You are a kind and merciful God, and you are very patient. You always show love, and you don't like to punish anyone. Now let me die! I'd be better off dead"*

Alienated people who are cut from cloth of obscurity but for the greater use of human, civil and or spiritual service must galvanize themselves together in community as God would allow. Even as a unified coalition this group will still be a marginalized rarity.

I remember a conversation that I had with my cousin the late Rev, Brandon McCray as he was a voice of inspiration to me. By chance we intersected with each other at the Super Walmart store near the potato chips and cashews as he went to greet me. "Hey Cuz" was his greeting to me. He went on to encourage me unbeknownst to him that I needed it as my efforts to be and become were a bit withdrawn that week. He simply said to me "little Cuz, I see you, keep pushing, you're just as good as anybody that's out right now." He was speaking of my music career. Now what he said may seem neutral and pre-worn to some. It wasn't only what he said, it was also who said it. Dr. McCray was a part of the rare constituency of the Preacher/Music Ministry hybrid as he was an internationally known and accomplished saxophonist. This means that he saw life from a similar view as I did. Dr McCray understood the politics, protocols and pressures that surrounded ministry and that consecration, but also like-minded fellowship would be key.

Figuratively speaking everyone with a call needs a Brandon McCray that will stand in the gap as a voice of hope. Some words you never forget the effect they have on you. In this case such reality was amplified after Evangelist McCray sadly became a Covid-19 mortal. Some people's advice is even more sound after they are gone. The person may (R.I.H/ Rest In Heaven), but their words carry the same acronym value but with a different tenure (R.I.H./ Resounding In Honor).

Here's a 'simple & plain' word from the Lord to me, that I feel led to share.

What happens to humans that jump off from an airplane while its landing or soaring? Most likely they become a mortal memory!

Alienated people don't fit into the cliques well. The cliques often conflict with their call as well as their hyper focused attention towards preparation of the work. I never felt at home when certain groups that my gifts assisted became opposed with another who were said to be serving the same Christ. When the glory would shift from kingdom purposes and pure motives so did my interest. I discovered something and through my own past mistakes I am compelled to share.

EXPLANATION:

We, the alienated, at times can have a tendency to conclude seasons before time that are uncomfortable, uncommon, unclear and simultaneously stretch us. (Ouch!) This hurts to admit but shame on me not to share the wealth of honesty even if brutal, especially if brutal can prevent fatal!

There can also be a tendency to prematurely initiate a season that desired but has red ▶ flags surrounding it. This is often done to secure having something to flex our passion towards. Something to own or control can reinforce feelings of adequacy, however that must not be the object of affection. As discussed earlier in the chapter this can cause a "Reroute". It's best to secure future acquisitions by enduring the process, even the painful parts.

INTERPRETATION:

Don't prematurely conclude or start a season with something or someone even if you know the season may be concluding or initiating. We must not in this season confuse our (ING) with our (ED): Land(ing) -vs- Land(ed).

The distance between the two is most often the difference maker. If you're trusting God to govern all things then you can't allow the behaviors of others or personal emotions to fog, cloud or usurp this reality. You can jump off the plane as shown while its landing and still perish. You can also allow it to land as it was independent of hurt avoidable death or "Reroute".

Alienation can be a menu item ordered by the Lord. However, it can be a DESERT ordered by people for your demise that God allows, ultimately to convert it into a DESSERT.

Marginalism, when In God's hand has a way of becoming a magnified miracle. This is what the chapter title refers to when it says alienation as a signal of awareness preparing you for "Acquisition". Acquisitions refers to what's acquired or obtained. This centers on the idea that alienation has a purpose, coupled with perks and a payoff when God's way remains the idolized direction of standard. That said, I'm reminded of a story of a distant mentor of mine who I met only once but was deeply encouraged by as it highlights how alienation overtime can accumulate into acquisitions.

In 1967 Gospel Artist and Songwriter Edwin Hawkins, penned the song "OH HAPPY DAY"_which to me was also an anthem of liberation to the direction of gospel music at that time.

While it earned him a Grammy Award, it was not without much controversy. It's not always what's said that hurts, but rather whose lips it came from. The same church that anointed him, also appealed for the dismissal of the song.

A group of local pastors petitioned to have it pulled from rock radio, and many Christians criticized the group for performing in mainstream venues. The song was marginalized as SECULAR, because of a muted piano, a drum track and crossover appeal. When the resistance from the church hit the fan, it caused a Global inquiry that put the song in controversial rotation, or very close to what we refer to as 'click bait'. Controversial in motive but tantalizing in sales as the advertising though adverse was accumulative towards acquisition.

The fame of the song to hit like a tidal wave; 500 copies were printed originally, but after the resistance, the song sold over 4 million copies.

There is a lesson here. Had the accusers known that their slander and attempted alienation would've pushed the song to a platinum level, then they would've SHUT THEIR MOUTH.

Yikes! (Preach Portley)

People have to remember as I've previously stated but must revisit "HAD THEY SHUT UP MAYBE YOU would have GIVEN UP, little did they know that their mouth became your MOTIVATION, MEDICATION & MUSCLE.

A-Flat in this chapter to me represented the importance of AQ/ Adaptability Quotient.

In the Pentecostal church there would be times then as well as in secular venues when you had to learn how to read your crowd. This determines your approach and how the effectiveness of your Adaptability skills would resonate with your audience musically. I learned that when popularity and personality had run its course then true relationships had an opportunity to be born, likewise what was artificial was exposed and decomposed.

Let me go further. As a musician, singer, artist and or preacher it's easier to live as the impact is more persuasive with a new audience. Some actual abuse this by consecutively offering the same presentation to new audiences. This works in such cases as long as the presenter knows that their growth is stunted with the abuse of serving frozen warmed up leftovers. I say this with a smile in my heart. The real work occurs when there's the same or similar audience who've already surpassed the wow factor of you. They are now supporters that you must now sustain to maintain their interest. For this to work the presenter (artist, singer, musician, preacher, dancer, poet, PowerPoint tech, etc.), now has to create relationships with that ongoing audience. Also, the presenter has to engage in the responsibility of providing upgraded material on a frequent basis that administers edification and pleasure to that ongoing audience. This requires Adaptability which is a skill set that is groomed over time. Work ethics and patience are crucial components to this.

As we close this chapter, I would like to leave a portion of words to a song made popular by Dewayne Woods entitled: "Let Go, Let God"

I couldn't seem to fall asleep

There was so much on my mind
Searching for that peace
But the peace I could not find
So then I kneeled down to pray
Praying help me please
But then he said you don't have to cry
'Cause I'll supply all your needs

As soon as I stop worrying
Worrying how the story ends
I let go and I let God
Let God have His way
That's when things start happening
When I stopped looking at back then
I let go and I let God
Let God have his way

There's so much going on
Sometimes I can't find my way
And often times I struggle
Struggle from day to day
I have to realize that it's not my battle
It's not my battle to fight
I have to know if I put it in your hands
That everything will be alright

Let go, let God
Let go, and let God

Let go, let God
Oh, let go and let God
Let go, and let God

Soon as I stop worrying
Worrying how the story ends
Then and only then can I
I can let go and I can let God
Let God have His way.

Source: Musixmatch
Songwriters: Paul Morton Jr

CHAPTER 15

Atomic Ascension

Okay family, I'm becoming saddened as our time together is reaching its expiration. We are in our final chapter as it's been a roller coaster for me. Some parts of this novel caused parts of my trauma wounds to resurface as at other times the spontaneous joy of laughter hit me like a blizzard. So, let's embrace the subject at hand as we take a vivid look at ATOM ASCENSIONS:

What's atomic is also explosive, rocket fueled and ready for a Supernatural soar.

Dissecting this we must know that a supernatural soar in most cases is pre-lubed by supernatural war.

Israel was brought out by the miraculous at such a level that, should they have changed their mind, death culprit by Pharaoh's tyranny would've been the only option.

Exodus 19:4 (NIV), *"You yourselves have seen what I did to Egypt, and how I carried you on eagles' wings and brought you to myself."*

It's much like Jobs' hedge, in Job 1:9-10 (ESV), *"Then Satan answered the Lord and said, "Does Job fear God for no reason? Have you not put a hedge around him and his house and all that he has on every side? You have blessed the work of his hands, and his possessions have increased in the land.*

The removal of that hedge and the Devil would've had his head. Let's juxtaposed the hedge for a minute. In the book of Ezekiel, the warfare was so high that without hedge God said that he would pour out his indignation to a point of consuming them.

Ezekiel 22:30-31 (KJV), *"And I sought for a man among them, that should make up the hedge, and stand in the gap before me for the land, that I should not destroy it: but I found none. Therefore, have I poured out mine indignation upon them; I have consumed them with the fire of my wrath: their own way have I recompensed upon their heads, saith the Lord God"*

So, in a season of Atomic Ascension the consequences of sin are more severe. This must be said because so many desire the ascending so much that the responsibilities and retribution are often overlooked.

Moses when hitting the Rock, cost him entry into the promised land. As a student of theology, I'd often venture to inquire as to why could the Israelites murder with their mouth and murmur in multiple complaints, yet they were granted admission into Canaan? It's because they were not the leader, nor did God award them the access to himself that Moses privileged to acquire.

We often forget to mention the encounter when Moses thought God's hot watered temper had cooled down as he asked him in the tone of a plaintiff for God to reconsider his verdict against him.

Deuteronomy 3:23-26 (NIV), *"At that time I pleaded with the Lord: "Sovereign Lord, you have begun to show to your servant your greatness and your strong hand. For what god is there in heaven or on earth who can do the deeds and mighty works you do? Let me go over and see the good land beyond the Jordan—that fine hill country and Lebanon." But because of you the Lord was angry with me and would not listen to me. "That is enough," the Lord said. "Do not speak to me anymore about this matter.*

In other words, Moses asked God again to go over and he said no!

Why would God hold his ground so firmly without budging against someone who he called a friend? It was because God doesn't operate off of personality but rather off of principles. Not only that, God has no peers. He called Moses friend as seen in Exodus 33:11a (KJV), *"And the Lord spake unto Moses face to face, as a man speaketh unto his friend. And he turned again into the camp"*

God never referenced him as his peer, as that would have made him a close equivalent. We must remember that even though we have a relationship with God that we still are his inferior as he is our "SUPREME SUPERIOR". God is preparing many for atomic upgrades. I see prophetic quantum leaps in the spirit propelling your advancement to highs unknown. You must beware that sin can recall your ascension. This includes carnal response too. All Moses did was respond to the people with the same energy that came for him, but his response shot himself in the foot as they drank the water that perused from the rock and later entered the land.

Your ascension must go beyond the air as stated in *Ephesian 2:2 (KJV), "Wherein in time past ye walked according to the course of this world, according to the prince of the power of the air, the spirit that now worketh in the children of disobedience:"*

What I mean is that according to Psalms 24:1 (KJV) it says, *"The earth is the Lord's, and the fulness thereof; the world, and they that dwell therein."*

This reveals that the earth and the world are not the same. The earth refers to the physical dry land mass as in the "Terra Firma". The world deals with the cosmos (kosmos /Greek) as it relates to kingdom order, structures and systems in the earth. Paul the Apostle in Ephesian 2:2 refers to air space.

As intercessors we must layer our prayers in such atomic reinforcements that the demonic air space wouldn't be able to afflict hindrances against them. This is why faith along with our constant confession and decrees is so important. Often it is in the air of the satanic where our prayers are held up. That why we have to speak to our mountains if they are going to move. Some things have to be spoken and not just felt or thought. It's like love. On my wedding anniversaries, I can't just love my wife, I must say it and demonstrate it. (*Let the church say Amen*) So it is with demonic warfare. How is this done?

This is achieved by way of what I call "THE BREAKERS ANOINTING".

The Breakers Anointing is an Authoritative Anointing…It does take sides. It takes over. It does not ask, it commands. It is not passive; it's sharply pointed and unapologetically persuasive. It has to be when you're against an enemy who intentions are annihilate as stated in John 10:10 (NKJV), "The thief does not come except to steal, and to kill, and to destroy. I have come that they may have life, and that they may have it more abundantly."

The word breaker means to break through! Breaking through hindrances, bondages, delays, and or strongholds unwarranted is the idea here.

Luke 13:11 records a woman that for 18 years was a victim of physical bondage.

She had a bent back; this was the only time the scriptures used the phrase "THE SPIRIT OF INFIRMITY" meaning it was beyond occasional but rather a consolidation of consecutive bouts of illness. Jesus then released the BREAKERS ANOINTING, which caused the infirmity to lose its grip declaring "Woman Thou Art Loosed". Immediately her back began to straighten up. He spoke it first, then manifestation followed. Some things that are out of alignment in your life are about to straighten up and be restored.

This visual here is a portrait of what the Breaker Anointing accomplishes. The Lord Himself Becomes Our Liquid Drano as the power of his name chokes up the HOLD THAT'S BEEN HOLDING YOU UP.

The Drano advertises its warranty as it states that it is guaranteed to work or it's free. No one is giving away money or putting it on the line unless they have utmost confidence in what or who they are advertising. This is how the Breakers Anointing works. It's guaranteed to unclog and rid all hindering spirits, and because "God is The Greatest Power We Shall Never Be Defeated". Hallelujah!

Here's a handful of scripture references that speak to this:

Jeremiah 23:29 KJV,_"*Is not my word like as a fire? saith the LORD; and like a hammer that breaketh the rock in pieces?*"

This analogy in Jeremiah is used to demonstrate the force of the BREAKER ANOINTING.

Micah 2:13 KJV, "*The breaker goes up before them; They break out, pass through the gate and go out by it. So their king goes on before them, And the Lord at their head.*"

This analogy is used by the prophet Micah to demonstrate gates of access, entry and refuge we have as leaders (the king) if we follow the Lord who's at the head.

Jeremiah1:10 KJV,_"*See, I have this day set thee over the nations and over the kingdoms, to root out, and to pull down, and to destroy, and to throw down, to build, and to plant.*"

This analogy of Jeremiah seems to observe how demolition proceeds reconstruction. This is crucial as God is saying that every situation doesn't merit restorative repair. Sometimes eradication before erection is what has to occur.

Isaiah 10:27 KJV, *"And it shall come to pass on that day, that his burden shall be taken away from off thy shoulder, and his yoke from off thy neck, and the yoke shall be destroyed because of the anointing."*

In the analogy, according to the Hebraic custom The FATNESS of the oxen would Break the yoke, then the oxen would step on the broken yoke and by default would destroy it rendering it usable. Likewise, is the BREAKERS ANOINTING.

We also saw this In Acts 12 when Herod vexed the church and threw Peter in Jail. The church prayed, and it invited the Angelic Assistance. The Angel of Deliverance operated in the BREAKERS ANOINTING chains of Peter Broke off.

Acts 12:6-8 KJV, *"And when Herod would have brought him forth, the same night Peter was sleeping between two soldiers, bound with two chains: and the keepers before the door kept the prison."*

"And, behold, the angel of the Lord came upon him, and a light shined in the prison: and he smote Peter on the side, and raised him up, saying, Arise up quickly. And his chains fell off from his hands."

"And the angel said unto him, Gird thyself, and bind on thy sandals. And so he did. And he saith unto him, Cast thy garment about thee, and follow me."

The angel did not walk out of the jail for Peter, Peter had to walk in that deliverance.

Walking In Your Deliverance Often Means Walking Away from Your Distraction.

(Preach Portley)

God is saying that this is not a season for believers to be PAMPERED, PETTED, PITIED, or PACIFIED, but rather PREPARED for war.

Our prayers must go higher, even to the level of the atomic as we were given insight to the nature of our resistances.

Ephesians 6:12 KJV, *"For we wrestle not against flesh and blood, but against principalities, against powers, against the rulers of the darkness of this world, against spiritual wickedness in high places."*

The enemies here are diabolical and can only be overruled in the Spirit with prayer.

There are 5 types:

Barkers: They talk well, they have the soundbites mastered as in knowing what to say hoping to instigate the opposition into fear. They were all bark; they had no real bite.

Fighters: These are better than barkers as they do have bite. They are motivated by action, theatrics, and activity. There's no real strategy and if they don't accidentally win, they quickly drift off into the dark abyss of isolation.

Soldiers: These are greater than fighters as they study the tyrant and tyraine as a strategy point. If they lose the battle they, do it in grace educating themselves on how they lose in order to prepare the relaunch of their comeback. They will be back!

Warriors: These are greater than soldiers as they have given themselves to the discipline of learning to win and learning how to lose. They study their enemies' weaknesses and perfect the accurate timing of attack. The warrior knows what battles to lose to secure winning the war.

Conquers: These are simply the winners of the War!

The Greek word for victory is the word Nike as in the name brand shoe.

From the noun νίκη (níkē, "victory")[1]

From the visual we see that the strings were tied up speaking to that of a unified mind and like-minded purpose pulling itself

---

[1] https://en.m.wiktionary.org

into alignment to prevent *falling* victim to demonic schemes. Then there's the tongues of the shoe that speak to the language of instruction uttered by the Spirit and only perceived in understanding by those connected to that source. There finally we see the thick soles for durability and pivot as well as the color red representing crimson stain for forgiveness.

A common denominator often made by believers is that many win the fight but lose the match! The thinner of the fight unleashed venom at the moment but the winner of the match's name is recorded and is etched in epochs time.

On September 22, 2013, two UFC light heavyweights duked it out for the championship. Challenger Alexander Gustafsson (blue trunks) squares off with Champion Jon Jones (black trunks). This was an epic thriller in every sense of the word but after 5 rounds of 5 minutes combining into 25 minutes of mortal combat the challenger Alexander Gustafsson by universal optics won the fight, but it was Jon Jones who won the match retaining both his title and record he had going into the fight. This was magnified immediately afterwards when the champion and winner of the contested match was immediately rushed to the hospital and was eventually greeted in love by the challenger who lost the match but won the fight.

I can say this briefly. We must not only be tougher than the enemy but also smarter than them too. The smarter opponent often is the winner, not the tougher fighter. This is why prayer and our approach to prayer is so important.

Prayer influences battle outcomes, it shifts molecules, subdues satanic structures, withstands demonic systems and changes the fragrance of atmospheres. Though powerful within itself, there are still levels to it. The question becomes,,. what is the determining force between a miraculous testimony that occurs eventually when compared to those that come suddenly? It is the level of prayer from the intercessor and where their spiritual acuity lies. Ascension of any kind requires some level of increased consecration. However, there are some ascensions that graduate level and become dimensions. In this case these are "Atomic Ascensions". No way can these occur without Divine mandate and assistance. People often covet and criticize such ascensions naturally but have no idea what it took to get there, and the continued intercession needed to maintain.

We see this with the Ascension of Jesus.

It happened so fast as he took 40 days engaging in infallible proofs.

Acts 1:3-4 (KJV), *"To whom also he shewed himself alive after his passion by many infallible proofs, being seen of them forty days, and speaking of the things pertaining to the kingdom of God:*

And, being assembled together with them, commanded them that they should not depart from Jerusalem, but wait for the promise of the Father, which, saith he, ye have heard of me."

After those 40 days it was as if he was just "ATOMICLY ASCENDED" into the heavens.

Acts 1:9-11 (NIV), *"After he said this, he was taken up before their very eyes, and a cloud hid him from their sight.*

"They were looking intently up into the sky as he was going, when suddenly two men dressed in white stood beside them. "Men of Galilee," they said, "why do you stand here looking into the sky? This same Jesus, who has been taken from you into heaven, will come back in the same way you have seen him go into heaven."

This is momentum that I believe God is preparing for you, not just an ascension, but with the adjective of ATOMIC attached to it. Listen beloved, as the Lord is preparing you for this, are you ready for what comes with this? Are you aware that these types of ascensions are what most desire but aren't prepared for how lonely it can get at the top? Are you ready for closest friends to possibly become your worst enemy simply because of the favor of God being demonstrated in you? Do you accept the distance from family that often accompanies atomic ascensions?

These are things that God knows if we are prepared or unprepared to handle and therefore shelves some while unseating others.

The world is in the midst of a mass Shaking and Awakening. Shaking is a biblical word often interchangeable with the word Shifting as seen in Hebrews 12:26-27 (NIV), *"At that time his voice shook the earth, but now he has promised, "Once more I will shake not only the earth but also the heavens." The words 'once more' indicate the removing of what can be shaken—that is, created things—so that what cannot be shaken may remain".*

The unknown writer of Hebrews is clear that what can be shaken will be shook while what cannot be shaken will remain. He's referring to a remnant. So, we are in a season where the lookalikes are being exposed and the true warriors advertised!

The Polaroid Camera was an era that predated Facebook, IG, TikTok, and Snapchat. It was the best thing out until future inventions replaced it. One thing that I recall about them is that the quality of the resolution was determined by how they were shaken.

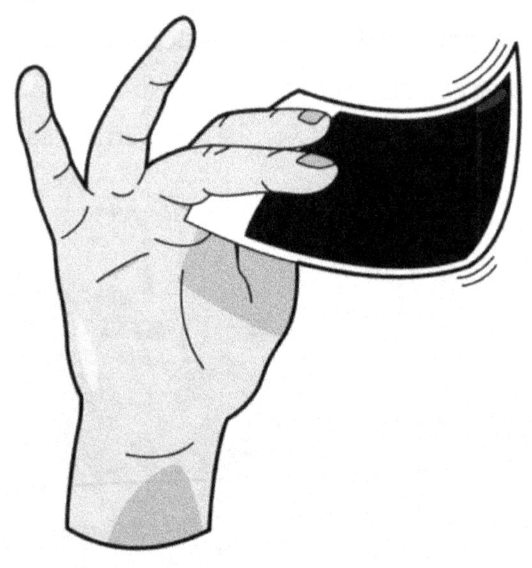

Likewise, the earth is undergoing a mass "shakening" and many pictures will survive the poses and snaps but won't survive the shaking. Let me say it another way,

"YOU WON'T MAKE THE FINAL TAKE IF YOU DON'T SURVIVE THE SHAKE."

In order for the universal church of the Lord Jesus to survive these times of mass Shakening,

We've got to get back our -- SATAN THE LORD REBUKE THEE!!

We've become too nice and too passive, we should honor Leadership as we are better with them than without them, but we are to obey the Lord!!

Just to name few but not limited to any....

*Ronald Reagans Remedies aided us, but only got us so far. They were good for that time.

*Obamas Opportunities were great & noteworthy but even a good Run, Runs Out!

Jimmy Carter's Cautiousness and Credibility was amazing just as Bill Clinton's Charismatic Clout was impressive, but they all had limitations!

*George Bush's Brains & Benevolence were a blessing; Trumps tenacity was often conversation worthy as was Biden's Bountifulness but after the laundry list of such amazing contributions what the world needs today is the "Blood of the Savior"

That keeping blood, that saving blood that healing blood, as reinforced in Revelation 12:11 (KJV), *"And they overcame him by the blood of the Lamb, and by the word of their testimony; and they loved not their lives unto the death"*

In order for the Atomic Ascension to work not only must we abort sin, but we must make sure that our callings are pure for the season you're in. Callings, careers, and commissions can change. Sometimes they can remain but the assigned territory to execute those functions can change. Sometimes both can change. Sometimes neither change but there is a need for spirit renewal and revival. Where would you rate yourself here? Where are you currently with your calling, career and or commission?

The Apostle Paul says something interesting in his epistle to the Ephesian church.

Ephesians 1:15-18 (KJV):

"Wherefore I also, after I heard of your faith in the Lord Jesus, and love unto all the saints, That the God of our Lord Jesus Christ, the Father of glory, may give unto you the spirit of wisdom and revelation in the knowledge of him:"

"The eyes of your understanding being enlightened; that ye may know what is the hope of his calling, and what the riches of the glory of his inheritance in the saints".

He was saying that our understanding is awakened when we know the hope of our call authentically. Riches and wealth also follow this. Of course, you aren't to chase wealth and riches but when operating in the right calling it will chase you.

Many of the callings of this age can come off as rehearsed, watered down, very thin in substance and goal oriented. Goals are good but we must not mix ministry vocation as a goal. I refer to them as "piñatas ordinations".

This is a visual of a Taco piñata. It has the appearance of beef protein, lettuce vegetables, dairy and corn shell. It looks very robust and appetizing on the outside but there are no nutrients on the inside, only sugar candy that will produce cavities. This resembles a spiritual vocation that's not real or a vocation that changed but the vessel called refused to pivot with the shift. When the piñatas are hit, the right tear causes everything in it to leak out. The external images portrayed are then exposed and discarded.

Your Atomic Ascension is closer than it's ever been. Get ready to be promoted as it will happen when least expected and at a speed unfathomable. (Receive this as the Word of The Lord).

A-Flat in this chapter causes me to retrospectively glance back at some of revival services that I was invited to play at in my earlier days. I'm talking about 20 plus years ago. There were times when the atomic surges of the anointing would overtake the atmosphere through me as I would play. All of a sudden, a radiant wind of God's Glory would hover over the place. I remember being afraid to cry. This was often! Honestly, I do know why. I was great at telling jokes outside of church and I feared that if I cried those, I joked on would then have ammunition on me.

This was before the social media age. This period lasted for a while, but the day came when real life happened, and opportunity had caught up with praise. Tears flooded my eyes and joy filled my heart as my life was transitioning from music-to-music ministry. I sat at the organ and began to weep and thank God for his goodness and choice of me. I wept as one who made up for the years, I held it back. These were the moments when the 4 to 5-minute scheduled songs would go 9 to 10 minutes because of the spontaneous personality of the anointing as the A and B selections converted over into unscheduled and undignified worship. This was not merely the skill and was much greater than musical improvisation. I call it "THE HOLY GHOST HIGH JACK" where God takes completely over, and needs are met. I knew from this point on that any barrier life threw at me that God's Spirit if I allowed would carry me through it.

Wow, I'm tearing up writing now because of God's goodness and because our time together has drawn nigh.

The final portion of lyrics I will leave you before we pray is a song entitled:

"I Give Myself Away" **by William McDowell**

Here I am

Here I stand

Lord, my life is in your hands
Lord, I'm longing to see
Your desires revealed in me

I give myself away
I give myself away
So You can use me

I give myself away
I give myself away
So You can use me

Take my heart
Take my life
As a living sacrifice
All my dreams all my plans
Lord I place them in your hands

I give myself away
I give myself away
So You can use me

My life is not my own
To you I belong
I give myself, I give myself to you
Oh oh my life is not my own
To you I belong
I give myself, I give myself to you

I give myself, Away
Source: *LyricFind*
Songwriters: *W McDowell*

Our time together has been something that I will cherish for the rest of my days. I am honored that our paths crossed and even more grateful for this opportunity to speak over you. Let's pray!

Holy God, you have been our compassionate liberator throughout the ages and from sand prints of time. Landmark upon landmark, decade by decade your faithfulness has served as a constant shield of protection aiding us through periods of economic hardship and industrial downturn lending accreditation to your resource sustainability. We thank you. Now I speak life to your people that as you are releasing some, restoring and reassigning others that you will favor them as it is your pleasure. We pray for utmost direction, precision of clarity and supernatural provision to pursue them in surplus form, now let the words of my mouth and the meditation of my heart Be acceptable in Your sight, O LORD, my strength, and my Redeemer.

May the grace our Lord Jesus, the love of God, and the sweet communion of the Holy Spirit rest rule and abide in us hence now and evermore,

Now unto him that is able to keep you from falling, and to present you faultless before the presence of his glory with exceeding joy. To the only wise God our Saviour, the glory and majesty, dominion, and power, both now and ever. Amen.

MICHAEL | MONICA | CARLTON | KRISTI | PRESTON | TIFANI | RAMON

A-FLAT